PRAISE FOR *MARRIAG*

Marriage Rebranded marks the debut of a ь..
earnest believer. Tyler Ward asks all the right questiuiɪ◡ ◡
and comes up with compelling answers. If you want to think more ɑeepıy
about marriage, more biblically, and more thoughtfully, this is the book
for you.

Gary Thomas, author of *Sacred Marriage* and *A Lifelong Love*

I am not a fan of "marriage" books because they tend to be formulaic and
boring. *Marriage Rebranded* is neither. Witty, entertaining, and thoughtfully
authentic, Tyler has delivered an unusually artistic conversation starter and
enhancer worthy of your time and attention.

William Paul Young, author of The Shack and Crossroads

In *Marriage* ome subject of
marriage wit ıumor. In a culture where ᵗ to erode, Ward
asks the big ate the mystery
of love.

Jonathan Jackson, actor, author, and musician

Tyler Ward cleverly and clearly uncovers some of the most commonly held
misconceptions of marriage. At a time when many singles and married couples have been confused by popular societal myths regarding relationship,
Marriage Rebranded sets a solid foundation to build godly relationships. We
highly recommend this book to singles and married couples alike.

Barry and Lori Byrne, marriage and family therapists,
authors of *Love After Marriage*

I just finished reading *Marriage Rebranded* and I'm blown away! Tyler Ward
isn't just teaching us how to dream, expect, and get more out of our
marriage—he has also raised the bar for what an advice book can and
should be. Wrapped in refreshing vulnerability, compelling storytelling,
and uncommon insight, *Marriage Rebranded* is a life-giving resource for
any marriage and an absolute must-read for young couples.

Chance Scoggins, Grammy-award winning producer and blogger

Marriage Rebranded offers an all-too-necessary re-vision for the working power of matrimony in a couple's life, while not shying away from the unanticipated realities that marriage brings out in each individual. Tyler gathers the best of the best in relevant marriage materials from a wide range of authors, teachers, and thinkers, to construct a beautifully renewed model of marriage, hand-painted from his own testimonies of trial and error.

Jared Black, speaker, writer, and theologian

The best artists often take the most common or familiar subjects and represent them in a way that unveils the divine essence within. In the following pages, Tyler Ward masterfully infuses the sacred colors back into the often tired, black and white world of holy matrimony. Whether single, newlywed, or seasoned in the art of marriage, the following pages are sure to enhance your view, grace your understanding, and strengthen your resolve to love more deeply.

Brady Toops, singer, songwriter

I'm honored to be one of the voices Tyler sought to speak into "rebranding" your marriage. But I think it's Tyler's wife, Analee's voice who makes the strongest case for why you should read this book. She writes, "I am incredibly thankful he (Tyler) has been so committed to finding the greatness in marriage and leading us toward it." That's EXACTLY where you want your marriage to go! So if you're ready to "rebrand" your marriage from good, ordinary, or even deeply disappointing, to simply "GREAT," this helpful, hopeful, hands-on book is a must-read.

John Trent, president of Strong Families and author of *The Blessing*

What I love about this book is that it speaks to your heart and your mind, which is rare in a lot marriage books. It's real, humorous, and insightful, which is also surprisingly refreshing. Love is a wild ride, as we know. It's ever changing and extremely crazy at times, but I am happy to say that I will have this book on board with me as a companion during its adventure. Very thankful for the truth in these pages, very thankful indeed.

Phillip Larue, Billboard Top 100 songwriter

Marriage Rebranded shifted our paradigms. It built a more realistic perspective about marriage and how to do love well. This book is a must-read that will build determination and hope in your hearts no matter the season of marriage you're in.

Colin Benward and Caitlin Crosby-Benward, founders of The Giving Keys

MARRIAGE REBRANDED

MARRIAGE REBRANDED

*Modern Misconceptions
& the Unnatural Art of
Loving Another Person*

TYLER WARD

MOODY PUBLISHERS
CHICAGO

All Scripture quotations, unless otherwise indicated, are taken from the *New American Standard
Bible®*, Copyright © 1960, 1962, 1963, 1968, 1971, 1972, 1973, 1975, 1977, 1995 by The Lockman
Foundation. Used by permission. (www.Lockman.org)

Scripture quotations marked KJV are taken from the King James Version.

Scripture quotations marked ESV are taken from *The Holy Bible, English Standard Version*. Copyright ©
2000, 2001 by Crossway Bibles, a division of Good News Publishers. Used by permission. All rights
reserved.

Scripture quotations marked MSG are taken from *The Message*. Copyright © 1993, 1994, 1995,
1996, 2000, 2001, 2002. Used by permission of NavPress Publishing Group.

Edited by Stephanie S. Smith of (In)dialogue Communications
Interior Design: Design Corps
Cover Design: Darren Lau
Cover photo of sparkler copyright © 2013 by Eduard Bonnin/Stocksy. All rights reserved.

Library of Congress Cataloging-in-Publication Data

Ward, Tyler.
    Marriage rebranded : modern misconceptions & the unnatural art of loving another person /
Tyler Ward.
        pages cm
        Summary: "Though statistics say marriage is a risky bet, many people still want to give it a try.
While other books may dwell on the downsides of marriage, Marriage Rebranded will help you see
the flipside of those ideas: Happily Ever After Isn't the Point, Marriage Isn't About Getting, Love
Isn't Something We Fall Into, and more. It's time to rebrand marriage, to take something great
that suffers from bad branding and give it the brand it actually deserves. If we let it, marriage can
change the world"-- Provided by publisher.
Includes bibliographical references.
    ISBN 978-0-8024-1183-9 (paperback)
    1. Marriage. 2. Interpersonal relations. I. Title.
HQ519.W37 2014
306.81--dc23

2014007220

We hope you enjoy this book from Moody Publishers. Our goal is to provide high-quality,
thought-provoking books and products that connect truth to your real needs and challenges. For
more information on other books and products written and produced from a biblical perspective,
go to www.moodypublishers.com or write to:

Moody Publishers
820 N. LaSalle Boulevard
Chicago, IL 60610

1 3 5 7 9 10 8 6 4 2

Printed in the United States of America

*"The mediocre teacher tells. The good teacher explains.
The superior teacher demonstrates.
The great teacher inspires."*
—William Arthur Ward

*To those who have
explained,
demonstrated,
and inspired this book . . .*

*JARED ETHAN BLACK
WILLIAM PAUL YOUNG
LORI and BARRY BYRNE
RABBI SHALOM ARUSH
GARY THOMAS
JOHN MEDINA
GARY CHAPMAN
JONATHAN JACKSON
PAUL E. RALPH
DUANE and KATHY WARD*

Thank you for painting a picture of marriage worth fighting for.

And to ANALEE,
*You're my Super Bowl, a daily reminder that life is good, and my
favorite choice. Thank you for putting up with my crazy experiments and my exceptionally slow learning curve as a husband.*

CONTENTS

CHAPTER ONE

A PICTURE WORTH FIGHTING FOR

My Story. A Modern Story.

I could feel the veins in my neck bulging.

The veins in my neck never bulge. I'm the emotionally unhealthy guy who internalizes everything—no matter how much the circumstance warrants a reaction.

The more she explains how my negligence of our relationship makes her feel, the more I want to jump in my truck and spend the weekend alone on the open road—neglecting our relationship.

Instead, I apply the proven tactic of bringing up unrelated isues as a means to make her feel shame. And voilà—she backs down and the night ends right on queue.

We then resort to our increasingly popular nightcap. I walk out slamming the door behind me for dramatic effect. She crawls under the covers in tears—but not before setting up her wall of pillows down the middle of the bed just to remind me, when I do come to sleep, that things are not okay.

Needless to say, Analee and I didn't come into marriage expecting, after only eighteen months, that screaming matches, excessive amounts of frustration, and pillow walls would become our norm. How did we get here? How does anyone get here?

To answer that question, we should probably start from the beginning.

IN THE BEGINNING.

I used to think I was a decently articulate guy, reasonably comfortable in my own skin. Then Analee would walk in the room.

Instantly, I had nothing but unintelligible things to say and a deep urge to be someone cooler and wiser and generally better than myself.

She was everything I wanted—everything I dreamed of in a woman. Electric personality. Exotically gorgeous. Lit up a room. World-travelled. She had a faith that was real and seasoned. She did most of the talking so I didn't have to. The list went on, and as it did, I became more and more convinced I wouldn't mind spending the rest of my life waking up next to her.

Of course, that meant she would have to feel the same way about me—a risky endeavor for any woman.

It took me six months of running in the same social circles to work up the courage to talk to her. Fortunately, I found the grit to mumble words in her direction and after a handful of texts—which may or may not have involved a few helpful Justin Timberlake lyrics—we found ourselves dating. Nine months later, I convinced her to marry me.

Saying "I do" to Analee is one of the better choices I've made in life. Anyone who knows us would concur and secretly wonder how I married so far up.

Our first year and a half of marriage felt like a perpetual sleepover with my best friend. We lived in a tiny cottage, in a quaint city, and bought a cute dog—all the makings of an absolute dream.

Then it happened.

It only took me eighteen months and a few blunted expectations to feel sincerely disappointed with marriage. There was nothing "wrong" with Analee. In fact, she was as lovely as she had ever been. This disappointment had little to do with her, and everything to do with my own misinformed ideas about marriage and their inability to support the very unnatural art of loving another person.

I had brought suitcases of misconceptions to the altar. And as these misconceptions were tested in the face of a very real relationship, we slowly but surely waved goodbye to our best friend slumber party and Norman Rockwell picturesque life.

Unresolved conflict soon became a staple of our relationship.

Failed expectations, yelling matches, and sleeping with a pillow fortress between us was not entirely new to this season. Yet these episodes seemed to be more frequent and less forgiving than in our first year of marriage.

We weren't supposed to be the ones in a perpetual fight. After all, we had all the tools to have a successful relationship. We knew each other's love languages. We had navigated conflict in the past. All throughout year one of newlywed life, we spent two hours every other week in counseling so we could avoid meltdowns like the ones we were now consistently experiencing. We were the couple who underlined and dog-eared their marriage books. Yet despite having all the tools at our fingertips, we often found ourselves too angry, exhausted, and generally uninterested in using them.

Something was missing. We both felt it. We both wondered why.

We exhausted those books early on, subtly believing that if we could expose ourselves to all of the best three-step formulas and tab them for easy reference, we could somehow avoid all of the ugly, uncomfortable realities of life with another human being.

But we couldn't. And as it turns out, we were never meant to.

As I took inventory of our relationship, the one thing I couldn't seem to find was a vision for our marriage worth fighting for. Don't get me wrong, I thought I knew what we were—by default—trying to build together: a happy life. A loving relationship. Two successful careers with a cushy joint bank account. A someday-family we could spend the rest of our lives driving to soccer practices, sending to college, and pushing out of the nest so we could retire into wild motor home adventures. But in the midst of a relationship that internally demanded so much, something told me a dream lifestyle wasn't the kind of vision that our marriage needed.

What we needed was a better picture of what marriage could be… one that didn't stop at a well-insulated life with a good partner and kids who don't do drugs. We needed a picture that answered in the deepest part of us *why* marriage is

important,

and valuable,

and worth investing into as much as it asks of us.

The interesting thing is that most of us today *have* a vision for marriage—whether or not we recognize it or can put it into words. We all bring to the table some construct of what we hope it will be. It's not a lack of vision that threatens many marriages today. What threatens our marriages is that many of our visions for matrimony have been crafted by modern and misguided ideas about love.

The next one hundred or so pages are about exposing these misguided ideas and exploring a vision of marriage worth fighting for.

MODERN MATRIMONY IS A STALE BRAND.

My general disillusionment with marriage is a popular place to land these days.

Sociologists say marriage is fundamentally broken.

Historians say it's outdated.

Progressives say it's not even necessary.

And tragically, statistics seem to say it's not worth it.

In America, one marriage ends every ten to thirteen seconds.[1] Almost half of the weddings you go to this year will celebrate the union of a couple who won't stay together. And if they do stay together for more than ten years, one out of every four of them will say they are unfulfilled in their relationship—but too comfortable to leave.[2]

The number of Americans saying "I do" has dropped each decade since the 1950s and cohabiting-but-unmarried partnerships have risen 1,000 percent over the last forty years.[3] "The question has become," as social scientist Andrew Cherlin says, "not why fewer people are getting married, but why so many are still getting married?"[4]

The disheartening statistics go on. Yet the statistics are also incredibly understandable.

Our parents' generation was handed a vision of marriage that apparently wasn't worth more than a 50 percent success rate.[5] They added their own dysfunctional patterns, as did any generation before them, and passed on this mediocre brand of what is supposed to be the height of human relationship.

As the infamous *Newsweek* article "The Case Against Marriage" put it, "Many grew up shepherded between bedrooms, minivans, and dinner tables, with stepparents, half-siblings, and highly complicated holiday schedules. You can imagine, then—amid incessant high-profile adultery scandals—that we'd be somewhat cynical about the institution [of marriage]."[6]

Then again, your parents may be about to celebrate their thirtieth anniversary of being happily married. Or maybe you've been fortunate enough to grow up with very functional and loving divorced parents. Or maybe you're just now entering marriage with nothing but the very best hopes and dreams. Regardless of the good, bad, or ugly exposure we've had personally to the institution of marriage, it's hard to deny that the path to marital disappointment is all around us. It's put on display every day—in the news, in celebrity relationships, in our friends' and coworkers' lives—and the truth is that even in the healthiest relationships, we will inevitably have moments with our spouse that cause us to entertain this exceedingly popular *misunderstanding*—the key word here—that marriage, as an ideal, is simply broken and disappointing.

However, the flip side of the divorce statistic tells a dramatically different narrative—one that perhaps we have not given enough attention.

MARRIAGE ISN'T BROKEN— IT'S SIMPLY MISUNDERSTOOD.

Yes, many marriages end in divorce.[7] The research is clear. But research also shows that when marriage "works," it *really* works. In fact, if cultivated, marriage is actually better for you on all fronts— physically, materially, and emotionally.[8] Studies show that healthily married people live longer, have better health, earn more money, accumulate more wealth, feel more fulfillment in their lives, enjoy a more satisfying sexual relationship, and have happier and more successful children than those who cohabitate or get divorced.[9]

Happiness? You are twice as likely to be happy if you stay married. And married people, in general, report lower levels of depression and stress than non-married.[10]

Health? Robin Simons, a sociologist at Wake Forest University, has done research that reflects that "married people overall do better on virtually every indicator of health and well-being."[11]

Sex? According to Linda Waite's research for her groundbreaking book with Maggie Gallagher, *The Case for Marriage*, over 40 percent of married women said their sex life was emotionally and physically satisfying, compared to about 30 percent of single women. The same trend is seen among men—50 percent of married men say they are physically and emotionally content versus 38 percent of cohabiting men. And 40 percent of married people have sex at least twice a week (not to mention those who have more!), compared to 20–25 percent of single and cohabiting men and women.[12]

The list of perks goes on, but only perpetuates the countertrend that marriage is not, in fact, disappointing. It's simply misunderstood. And we as a modern society seem to be largely unaware of its unique purposes.

IT'S TIME FOR A REBRAND.

Just as Analee and I were entering the painful epiphany that our marriage was missing something, we were invited to a friend's home for a "marriage day." We spent the day hearing timeless perspectives and honest reflections on marriage from older, more seasoned couples, and with every story they shared, a bit more color filled my picture for what marriage could be.

This day at a friend's home challenged my paradigm of matrimony. It painted just enough of a new picture that I couldn't help but want more. It marked the beginning of a personal journey to cultivate a vision of marriage worth fighting for.

It's a journey I'm still on today and a journey in which I'd love for you to join me.

I've spent the last three years putting the most basic assumptions about modern marriage to the test. Along the way, I've interviewed three *New York Times* bestselling authors, a molecular biologist devoted to family development, a prime-time TV star, a personality psychologist, two marriage therapists, and several couples whose relationships I simply admire. I've exhausted resources by Israeli Breslov rabbis, modern sociologists, sex therapists, Orthodox priests, university professors, and Christian counselors. And perhaps most importantly, my wife and I have explored these various ideas we've come across by conducting several experiments in our own marriage—every one of which has helped us change our marital narrative and learn the very unnatural art of loving another person.

I began sharing some of my experiments and findings over a year ago and was astonished at the responses. My first article on the subject, "3 Things I Wish I Knew Before We Got Married," was shared online over 350,000 times and the conversations started by readers clued me in to a few things.[13]

I've noticed I'm not alone in my desire for a new brand of marriage. In fact, I'm walking alongside a vast amount of people—like you—who aren't interested in accepting "marriage as usual."

I've noticed that most of us want something more from marriage than some quick fix for loneliness or romantic obsession or a tool of self-fulfillment. We want to invest ourselves deeply and see a deep return.

I've seen that many of us believe God created marriage for more than the American dream and idyllic family Christmas card. We want to know what He originally designed it to be.

Most of us know there's more to life than happiness. Instead, we want a version of marriage that actually deals with the realities of life in radical proximity with another person.

We all want to see the end of broken homes and raise children who grow up emotionally connected and confidently commissioned into adulthood.

We want relationship. Real, challenging, relationships that don't just enrich our lives, but play a role in showing the world a better way of life.

In the end, we want a better vision for marriage—one that answers in the deepest parts of us *why* we stay married—a vision that's worth fighting for.

I have no intention of spending the next few chapters handing you a step-by-step formula to a better marriage. You can pick that up from your local Walmart. I simply want to paint a picture of marriage that's worth endlessly investing into.

Join me on this endeavor and we'll talk about four misconceptions about love that accompany modern marriage—happiness, me-centricity, falling in love, and privatization. My hope is that by the end of this book, we'll have replaced them with timeless truths that will play a leading role in writing a better marriage narrative for us all.

However, before we jump in, here are five thoughts—in no particular order—that may help us get started.

1. Different strokes for different folks

This book is written under the assumption that if we want to change our reality, we must first change our own minds. Accordingly, we'll use three types of content.

 Mindset. These sections deal with debunking common misconceptions and offering a better way to see marriage.

 Best Practices. These sections suggest practical ways to help walk out the proposed mindset shifts.

 Case Studies. These sections document real-life experiences, primarily through interviews, of those who have seen these mindsets and best practices make a difference.

These three chapter elements are for people like me whose mood often dictates whether they want to chew on deeper ideas and philosophy, acquire practical life tools, or get proof via real life accounts. My hope is that when all three elements converge, a greater vision for marriage will start to come together.

2. Reflection helps

If you would like to dig deeper than this book has the page space to go, I've produced a downloadable PDF with questions as you read for personal or group reflection. It also includes suggested experiments and tools to try on your own. To download, simply visit www.tylerwardis.com/marriage-rebranded-reflections.

3. Formulas are for institutions

Don't be fooled by the term "Best Practices." I'm not suggesting a one-size-fits-all approach to marriage. These are simply practical insights and suggestions I've come across that have proved worth some experimentation.

Though we'll read plenty of cause-and-effect stories throughout the book, let's be clear that every relationship is profoundly unique. The success or failure of every relationship is a combination of many variables. The goal of this book is to look at a few of those variables from several different perspectives—not to offer a comprehensive guide. If you're looking for a way to avoid the process of trial and error required in developing any real relationship, there are plenty of books out there offering A + B = C. However, this is not one of them. Comprehensive formulas are for institutions, not relationships. And I think what we're all after is the latter.

4. My wife is going to join us

I've invited my wife into our time together. At all the right moments, she'll offer her own brilliant thoughts and perspectives.

5. Why I wrote this book

Let's be honest. If I picked up a book about marriage by an author who had only been married for five years, I'd be skeptical too. In our digital age when seemingly anyone with access to Wikipedia can become an overnight guru, I'd be apprehensive to read on as well. If I'm being honest, I initially turned down the request to write this book because of this exact stigma. However, after months of feeling drawn back to the project, here are two reasons I decided to write it.

One, I'm an expert. But only if by "expert" we mean what physicist and Nobel prize winner Niels Bohr means by it: "An expert is a person who has made all the mistakes that can be made in a very narrow field."[14] In fact, one could say this book is largely inspired by the documentation of all my mistakes in marriage, identifying the bad ideas behind them and attempting to replace them with better ones—key word here being "attempting." My wife would be the first to tell you that just because I may be writing about a beautiful picture of marriage does not mean I'm not in a long and challenging process to cultivate it in my own relationship.

But she can say it far better than I:

Analee's Point of View. *Marriage is the beautiful, messy at times, unfolding of two people in which our growth is never meant to stop. No matter where we are in this lifelong process, WE ARE ALL learning. And there's no question that I have my share of growing to do. But let's just say that the running family joke—that Tyler coined—throughout this writing process was that he couldn't make me his priority because he was too busy WRITING about making me his priority. In all seriousness though, I am incredibly thankful he has been so committed to finding the greatness in marriage and leading us toward it. I've never expected him to be perfect, but to watch him stay open and devoted to the process has been everything a wife could dream.*

I will be opening the good, bad, and ugly of our married life to you with the hope that you might see a bit of yourself in our story, or at least find a slightly better way to develop your own story. But in many ways, I'll simply be a guide to an exploration of ideas and suggestions posed by far more experienced people than I. Most of whom (they're all listed on the dedication page) took the time to sit with me, share life with me, and show me another piece of the beauty of this thing called marriage.

And two, I couldn't not write this book. The statistics are one thing, but I've watched nine young couples in the past two years walk away from their marriages. No doubt you've watched the painful process of marriages falling apart in the lives of friends and family, as well. And while it's true that the decision to end each marriage was unique, I would venture to say many if not most of these relationships were severed under the influence of bad ideas they've inherited about matrimony.

Don't get me wrong—I'm not saying divorce is universally wrong. Or that I am some sort of hero, here to rescue our current state of matrimony. What I'm saying is simply that, after watching several friends have their relationships destroyed by modern yet misinformed ideas about marriage, I couldn't *not* write this book.

So regardless of how broken your ideas about marriage are or are not, or how functional your marriage is or isn't, let's start over together. Let's wipe our slates clean and become apprentices to this thing called matrimony—or as I've come to know it, the very unnatural art of loving another person.

CHAPTER TWO

CARVING TO THE SKIN

Happily Ever After Isn't the Point

> *"Marriage is a school of sanctity."*
> *—Martin Luther*

Amanda did everything "right." She'd been reading relationship books since she was twelve and only dated when the prospect had the potential for marriage. Sam and Amanda spent the first year of their marriage settling into a new town, buying their first home, and starting their traditions of weekly dinner, a movie date, and late nights drinking wine on the back porch.

It was the beginning of a dream come true—or so she thought.

Sam took a new job fourteen months into their marriage, requiring more travel and late nights even when he wasn't on the road. Amanda quickly felt the loss but learned to cope with their new life. She supported him in his career by learning to require less of him and offering him space as he needed. As the demands of work became more intense for Sam, the weekly date nights became less frequent. Neither of them seemed to notice.

Three years and seven weeks after they exchanged vows, Amanda sat in our living room a couple weeks after Sam filed for divorce. As she shared about their short married life together, her sadness was only rivaled by her confusion about Sam's choice.

"We started so strong . . . He was such a great husband . . . I couldn't wait to see him as a father . . ."

Sam's story was a bit different. "There's no question in my mind that we were in love at the beginning," he said. "We had some of the best moments together. But as time passed, it's as if we became indifferent. I felt nothing when I left for a trip and nothing when I came home. *We just weren't happy anymore.*"

Unfortunately Sam and Amanda's story is a common one today. Many fall in love. Get married. The *happiness* that once validated this love inevitably fades. And many find themselves lost and confused.

In our modern era, you and I are led to believe that happiness is a worthy guide in life and that—in one way or another—we have some sort of inalienable right to experience it. As we'll see, our culture's obsession with being happy often makes it far more natural for us to love happiness more than we ever love another human. And though being happy is a very real by-product of a healthy relationship, this inflated value we give to it makes us vulnerable to missing one of the more beautiful purposes of marriage altogether. We're about to explore this in depth, but first, we need to reevaluate our misled ideas about happiness.

Stanley Hauerwas, an American theologian and Duke University professor, articulates here the bottom line: "Destructive to marriage is the self-fulfillment ethic that assumes marriage and the family are primarily institutions of personal fulfillment."[1]

I learned this lesson like I learn most things in my life: the hard way.

THE CHRONOLOGY OF A MODERN HEDONIST.

1989. My mom tells me I can't have another piece of blackberry pie at our family reunion. I happen to like blackberry pie very much, always have. To this day, she still recalls me uncharacteristically crying to the point of convulsing for an inappropriate amount of time.

1999. I find the new pinnacle of human existence after kissing my first girlfriend. She dumps me a few months later, and for weeks I'm convinced all of life's happiness is behind me.

2001. I experience God for the first time and read that He wants me to have life to the full. I tell my friends that I've found the key to happiness and invite them to join me. It didn't take me long to realize that even this kind of happiness came with a price that I often wasn't willing to pay.

2003. I'm not happy in the American suburbs, so I move to Kosovo, a recently war-torn nation where I hope finding the meaning of life will make me smile more than four years at a state college or a corporate gig. I drink a lot of coffee, make a lot of friends, but come home a year later with no sense of lasting fulfillment.

2007. Since I was a kid, I've wanted to live on the West Coast. So after college, I jumped into my car with $800 in my pocket and drove to LA. I lived in the Hollywood Hills, worked a job that had me traveling the world for free, and only occasionally found myself fulfilled.

2008. I meet a beautiful half-Filipino, half-Swedish actress in Hollywood. She loves God and kisses extremely well. After nine months of dating, I eventually convince her to marry me and we begin our happily ever after.

2011. Though I happened to marry my favorite person on earth and the first couple of years of our relationship are a dream, I'm now certain that nothing in life has ever made me more frustrated than marriage. It often feels as if just when I think I've given all I can possibly give, it somehow finds a way to ask for more.

The worst part of it all is that most of my wife's demands aren't unreasonable. One day she expects me to stay emotionally engaged. The next, she's looking for me to validate the way she feels. The list goes on—but never ventures far from things she perfectly deserves as a wife. Unfortunately for her, meeting her very valid needs at the expense of my own didn't play nice with my idea of "happily ever after."

Though I've been largely unaware of it, most decisions I've made in life have been subtly influenced by my pursuit of happiness. Maybe the same is true of you. It's human, after all—to want to be happy.

In fact, it's probably a bit more human than we think because the roots of our modern obsession with happiness reach deep into history.

A HISTORICAL SNAPSHOT OF MARITAL HEDONISM.

The Garden and Misaimed Desires. The hope of finding happiness through getting married is nothing new. According to biblical history, it reaches back to the beginning of human nature after an incident involving an apple and a mistake.

When introducing the consequences of Adam's fruit-tasting endeavor, God made it clear to Eve that . . .

"Your desire will be for your husband, and he will rule over you."[2]

This statement marked the first moment in history when a human being would not look to God for wholeness. Now, men and women both would try to find their fulfillment in another person or in the works of their hands. This marked a massive shift in what it meant to be fully human post-garden and it effectively began the perpetual slide toward the make-me-happy brand of marriage or singleness we find ourselves chasing today.

Skip several thousand years.

Free Market Capitalism and Happiness-Based Love. Modern consumerism offers an abundance of choices for anything in life, which, as psychologists have noted, can create problems for relationships.[3] With more choices come more progressive filters to help us make those choices. And the most popular of these filters today is known as the inherent rights of every American to life, liberty, and the pursuit of happiness. Necessity is no longer the issue when trying to determine which car to buy or restaurant to eat at. That's why, whether we are aware of it or not, most decisions many of us make from day to day are often made through the lens of a simple yet telling question: "What will make me happiest?"

In this consumer-like quest for happiness, it is easy to make marriage more about what makes us happy than the object of our affection.

Hollywood and Happily Ever After. As soon as we're able to understand bedtime stories, Cinderella and her friends tell us that love is about happiness. As we become teens, Hollywood takes up Cinderella's campaign inundating us with the idea that marriage—and sex—is our gateway into happily ever after.

Many of us then spend our dating relationships subconsciously asking if this one could be "The One" we get to dance with in the rain and make passionate love to for the rest of our lives. It's not until months into marriage that most of us realize Disney and Hollywood were full of it. At that point, our frustration with Cinderella is only rivaled by the disillusionment we feel in our marriage.

Obviously, I'm stereotyping and exaggerating the point. But social and scientific observations confirm this phenomenon, as well. According to a recent study, 67 percent of unmarried people believe they'll one day find their soul mate—an ideal largely perpetuated by Hollywood—and the same study shows that those who inherently expect this happily ever after are 150 percent more likely to divorce.[4] Additionally, science proves that the happy feelings in early stages of love have been proven to be a consistent neurochemical reaction, which biology calls the state of infatuation. This reaction—and all of the exhilarating emotions it offers young lovers—can't sustain itself any longer than twenty-four months, confirming that the unnatural reality of life in marriage can't hide behind happiness-based affection for very long.[5]

This is nothing new to you if you're a married individual. Like Sam and Amanda, anyone who has braved the commitment can validate that marriage doesn't always feel like the meeting of soul mates, nor is it always butterflies and sipping wine on the back porch. Marriage can at times feel more like exactly what it is: the very unnatural, and sometimes unhappy, reality of two unique people— with all of their beauty and dysfunction—attempting to love each other and navigate life together.

Sadly, many couples get stuck on these unnatural times. We are products of a culture that brings the hope of never-ending happiness to a relationship that isn't designed to *primarily* make us happy. As a result, we end up severely disappointed.

I'm certainly not assuming that all of us have bought into Cinderella's happiness-based hopes. But for those of us who have brought expectations of marriage being happy and easy—whether or not we're aware of them—it may be time to reevaluate. Perhaps it's time we realize that even though happiness has proven to be a very real result of a healthy marriage, true love has a far more significant purpose in mind.

THE MICHELANGELO EFFECT.

As legend tells it, the story of Michelangelo and his sculpture of *David* has something to say to us about what marriage is really for.[6]

As Michelangelo walked the art market, he passed a stone that had sat for some time, unwanted by anyone. Apparently several artists had tried to use the stone previously but found it had too many veins to produce anything of value. As Michelangelo walked by this rejected rock, he claims the stone spoke to him saying that David was inside of it. As he inquired about its price, the shop owner gave him the stone for free—simply wanting to free up space for a more sellable piece.

Michelangelo used the friction between his chisel and the rock to chip away—piece by piece—at this "useless" stone. Michelangelo didn't sculpt like other sculptors. No, he didn't believe he was creating something from nothing. Instead, he believed his slow, deliberate chiseling actually liberated what was already inside of the stone. He saw beautiful figures beneath the surface and considered it his responsibility as an artist to simply set them free.

Michelangelo described his unorthodox sculpting philosophy saying, "Carving is easy. You just have to go down to the skin and stop."

Two years of chiseling later, Michelangelo had set David free—and in the process, he sculpted this unlovely piece of rock into one of history's most renowned pieces of art.

I think there's more truth about marriage in this story than in most of our modern ideas about relationships. Marriage isn't, in fact, our gateway to happily ever after. It's more like a chisel in Divine hands. And though there's plenty of friction involved, it's designed to chip away at all the dysfunction in our lives and free the beautiful statues inside.[7]

Interestingly, the Bible seems to agree with this picture that Michelangelo's carving philosophy offers us. In fact, if you're ever wondering who you can blame for this chiseling sensation in your marriage, Adam—the first human in the Bible—is your guy.

A HEALING FIRE.

It all started when the first human on earth decided to name his wife after a hazardous chemical reaction.

After having just been introduced to the only other human being on earth, he says, "She shall be called *ishshah*—woman, because she was taken out of *ish*—man."[8]

Ish and *ishshah*. I assume that though they have a certain ring to them, these won't be topping your list of names for future kids. Even so, they paint a picture about marriage that answers many of our modern questions.

To start, both words are derived from the root word and Hebrew character *esh*, which means *fire*.[9]

This means that the original word picture we have for the relationship between a man and a woman is an all-consuming, tireless-in-nature, potentially hazard-creating fire. And though this picture lends itself to the modern concept of heated romance or passionate love, the Bible consistently points to a different purpose of fire.

Fire happens to be one of the Bible's primary metaphors for purification and personal development.

Jesus promised us, for example, that "everyone will be salted with fire."[10]

God points to the purpose of fire when He says, "I will put [them] into the fire, and refine them as one refines silver."[11]

King David, too, alludes to the intention of fire when he reflects in the Psalms, "We went through fire and through water, yet you brought us out into a place of abundance."[12]

It would seem that the relationship between two spouses—fire—as depicted by biblical accounts, is a source of personal refinement, designed to play a significant role in one's process of growth and maturity. But hang with me—the biblical picture gets better.

In the New Testament, Paul the apostle goes on to compare love in marriage to the love Jesus showed humanity. He says (emphasis mine):

> Husbands, love your wives, just as Christ also loved the church and gave Himself up for her, so that He might *sanctify* her [literally, purify her internally by the reformation of her soul], having cleansed her by the washing of water with the word, . . . having no spot or wrinkle or any such thing; but that she would be holy and blameless.[13]

This idea was beautifully expressed in a recent Orthodox Christian wedding we attended. During the ceremony, they acknowledged that Jesus did everything He did—including death on a tree—for our salvation. Then the priest looked at the couple and, borrowing Paul's comparison of marriage to Jesus' love, said, "You've been given to one another for the other's salvation." Not salvation in the sense that only-Jesus-can-save, the priest clarified, but the kind of salvation that's alluded to by the original Greek word *soteria*— meaning one's holistic healing, deliverance, and prosperity.[14]

Now that's a picture of marriage worth fighting for.

Marriage is actually about you and your spouse's holistic healing, deliverance, prospering, and growth. And similar to our former picture from Michelangelo, the Bible alludes to this unnatural relationship as a sort of tool in Divine hands to help us become increasingly beautiful—increasingly our best and brightest selves.

HAPPINESS < BEAUTY.

So what about this modern idea of happiness? Does it have a place or do we abandon the idea altogether to embrace the refining fire of marriage?

Not at all. Happiness is a very real result of a healthy marriage. Even modern social research shows that marriage historically offers more happiness than singleness or divorce.[15]

However, as we've seen from Michelangelo, Adam, and Paul, happiness is not the primary goal of your marriage. Becoming more beautiful by becoming your best self—more loving, joyful, peaceful, patient, kind, faithful, gentle, self-controlled—is the goal.

Marriage—like fire—can be an all-consuming and potentially painful substance. But also like a fire, it can refine us. And like a chisel liberating the figures inside of a rock, as it would seem, marriage is a tool that the Divine uses to make us beautiful.

Dan Allender and Tremper Longman, the authors of *Intimate Allies*, explain this paradox well: "Marriage is where depravity is best exposed . . . and because it, more than any other relationship, bears more potential to draw our hearts to heaven, it can more readily give us a taste of hell."[16]

I know that marriage can be one of the more challenging things we experience in life. And I know that at times, it demands far more than we feel we can give. I know there are moments when walking away seems like the only sane and rational thing to do. Yet I also know that marriage multiplies what we can become—both as individuals and as couples.

Marriage, even though it will introduce us to some of life's most arduous moments, has brilliant intentions in mind. It's unapologetically interested in chipping away at our dysfunctional thoughts, patterns, and postures in life and inviting us—and our spouses—to become the best version of ourselves.

When we remember this brilliant intention to liberate us—the beautiful statues trapped within our own mess—we begin to see a hopeful view of the relationship, even in its darkest times.

This vision of marriage takes the expectation off of our spouses to make us happy and re-creates the expectation that our marriage exists to help us grow.

It turns our focus from personal fulfillment to mutual personal development.

It exchanges our goal of happiness for the far more valuable goal of wholeness.

And yet . . .

As any growth in life, our "becoming" is dependent upon our choices and engagement. Once we understand this unique intention of marriage, the journey now becomes about learning how to participate in the liberation process.

LOOK IN THE MIRROR

How Your Spouse Helps You Become More Beautiful

*"One of the best wedding gifts God gave you was a
full-length mirror called your spouse. Had there been a card
attached, it would have said, 'Here's to helping you
discover what you're really like!'"*
—Gary and Betsy Ricucci

*"[Marriage] is the merciless revealer, the great white search-
light turned on the darkest places of human nature."*
—Katherine Anne Porter

I used to think I had my stuff together. Then I got married and quickly realized that I was simply undisturbed. Of course, I didn't stay undisturbed for long. But as it turns out, I was never meant to.

When we see that marriage is actually a divine tool for our holistic healing—this in itself is a life-altering truth. It's often even more than we signed up for—because it implies that our spouse is a God-given gift to help us "work out [our] own salvation."[17] It implies that regardless of his or her own jagged edges or even lack of intentional participation, our spouse is a chisel in Divine hands used to liberate us into becoming our best, beautiful selves.

THE MIRROR PHENONENON ACCORDING TO A KING AND A JEWISH RABBI.

One of the especially unique dynamics of this new—and often ironic—role our spouse assumes is what Solomon of the Bible alludes to when he says, "As in water face reflects face, so the heart of man reflects man."[18]

Shalom Arush, a Jewish rabbi and counselor, paints the picture of what I like to call the mirror phenomenon even more clearly. He says, "You didn't get married to correct your spouse. You got married to be corrected, by using your spouse as a mirror."[19]

I know. I didn't buy it either. The suggestion that she—with her free choice, separate past, and unique set of issues—was a mirror for me to see and deal with my own issues felt far-reaching and irrational at first. Yet after experimenting with the idea, my practical experience seems to agree with the rabbi's bold idea.

To the open-minded, here are a few pieces of advice I've been given that are worth experimenting with when it comes to this mirror phenomenon. In fact, the more I've tinkered with them, the more obvious it becomes that I really do wake up every morning next to a mirror—and she shows me the good, bad, and ugly.

1. Don't criticize—internalize

In *The First Two Years of Marriage*, Kathleen and Thomas Hart write, "Sometimes what is hard to take in the first years of marriage is not what we find out about our partner, but what we find out about ourselves." They give the example of a woman who has been married about a year, who says, "I always thought of myself as a patient and forgiving person. Then I began to wonder if that was just because I had never before gotten close to anyone. In marriage, when John and I began . . . dealing with differences, I saw how small and unforgiving I could be. I discovered a hardness in me I had never experienced before.'"[20]

If we look in a mirror and see that our shirt is wrinkled, we don't iron the mirror. No, we iron our shirt.[21]

It's the same with our spouse.

Internalizing is all about taking inventory of the things our spouse does that we've been quick to criticize or be annoyed by in the past and to ask, "How might my spouse's action or attitude be a reflection of my own dysfunction in the way I treat them?" The point is to transmute the very natural critique of our spouses into a self-evaluation that inevitably identifies broken thought and character patterns within us.

2. Don't try to fix him or her— take 100 percent responsibility

Marriage is *not* a fair deal and has little to do with equality. Though a popular sentiment, you don't simply take 50 percent of the responsibility for the relationship and expect your spouse to meet you halfway. From my observation, the healthiest marriages are the ones when both spouses fully own the relationship and take 100 percent responsibility for its condition.

The mirror phenomenon tells us that our spouse's dysfunction is not our responsibility to fix. Once we resist critiquing and make the correlation between their actions and something that needs to change in us, our job is to simply own our issue and fix us—to take 100 percent responsibility.

"Every married individual should feel," says Rabbi Shalom Arush, "that he or she alone bears the responsibility for peace in the home. Neither should police the other because a person that's occupied with finding fault in someone else fails to see his or her own faults."[22]

3. Watch your marriage change

"A fundamental law of relational theory," renowned psychiatrist Marina Benjamen reflects, "is that when any part of a system changes, the entire system—meaning all other parts—will be forced to change in response."

So what does this look like in marriage? She continues: "What this means in a marriage is that if I create a change in my own attitude and behavior, my spouse and the marriage itself will automatically be forced to change. This is a powerful truth to embrace but, unfortunately, most of us are so busy blaming our partners for their shortcomings that we neglect to assert our power to create the very changes we want."[23]

The best part about the mirror phenomenon is that, according to relational theory, the more we fix *ourselves*, the more our spouses change as well.

Marriage is committed to making both you and your spouse more beautiful, more functional, more vibrant people. And the sooner you accept that you wake up every day next to a mirror exposing all of your personal good, bad, and ugly, the sooner you will begin to take advantage of marriage's beautifying intentions.

FEEL THE FRICTION
How to Leverage Conflict for Good

"What counts in making a happy marriage is not so much how compatible you are, but how you deal with incompatibility."
—Leo Tolstoy

We all bring our baggage of bad choices, unhealed hurts, and ungodly beliefs to the marriage altar. Unfortunately, most of us—

including me—have no idea we're carrying this baggage until the covenant is made and the chisel starts chipping.

Conflict in marriage isn't a fun pastime for anyone. And though everyone has their own way of dealing with it, we must learn to leverage conflict in our relationships as an opportunity for growth. Why? Because without friction, those beautiful figures inside the rock won't ever have the chance to exist.

Jared Black is a speaker, author, and long-time friend and mentor.[24] In fact, he and his wife were the ones who hosted the marriage day that proved so important for Analee and me.

Recently I was spilling to Jared about the latest challenges in my and Analee's marriage—most of which revolved around tripping up each other's same old emotional land mines to disastrous effects. He was patient with me as I divulged our situation. When I was finished, he shared a play on words that changed everything for Analee and me in moments of conflict.

Enter Jared.

"My wife and I have discovered that our primary goal isn't learning to be married in a static sense so much as learning the art of marrying our own individual responses, desires, and efforts in any present moment.

"It usually looks like this: When we have a conflict, it is most often caused by a difference in the way we see a certain situation—unspoken expectations that aren't met, or general frustration at the way the other person handled something. We each solved whatever situation is now in question in our own, individualistic way; through our own lenses, valuing in our decision and actions only what was important to us individually.

"What is needed to accomplish the marrying of lives at that moment is to practice a method of resolving (read: *re-solve*) the situation through communication. Since it is clear that I have solved the situation a certain way and she has solved it a different way, then it becomes equally clear that on that particular issue, we now have an invitation to marry one another again. This is nothing to freak out about, but something to verbally acknowledge so that the work of re-solving can produce the intimacy that only the ongoing marrying of our two individual lives can bring."

I had never heard anyone describe conflict this way. Jared went on...

"The practice of re-solving marital issues revolves around learning to communicate well with your spouse. This takes practice. Two individuals are almost always terrible at this at first. Most unresolved issues in marriage stem [from] each person's inability to effectively hear what the other person is saying, and more importantly why they are saying it. Ironically, quality communication begins not by being a good talker, but by becoming a great listener.

"Think about it. Most conflict revolves around each person trying their hardest to be heard! Steph and I now jokingly say that the first one of us to hear the other wins the argument. Why? Because it is only by focusing on what the other is saying—getting into their head, seeing the values that were driving their decisions and actions in the moment—that we can finally get about the beauty of marrying our two individual worlds into a shared, exciting world of marriage."

Exit Jared.

With Jared's advice on seeing conflict as an opportunity to grow even closer, Analee and I began to see changes—some small, some radical—in our marriage. I'm confident this perspective can do the same for you.

In the end, marriage—like fire—is designed to pull all our inner dysfunction to the surface of our lives, refine it, and help us grow. When we're willing to see the rougher parts of marriage in this light, this friction quickly becomes a gift that constantly invites us into a fuller and more fulfilling experience of life together.

And if you were to ask me, that's a far better deal than happily ever after on a white horse.

CHAPTER THREE

REAL ROMANCE

Consumers Don't Make Good Lovers

> *"When two selfish people get married,*
> *you've got two ticks and no dog."*
> *—Unknown*

"She changed once we got married."

"We both had the right to be happy, and neither of us were."

"Steven always asked about how I was doing . . . My husband hasn't asked in years. It just felt nice to be thought about."

"He used to pursue me. Then we got married."

"He never made the effort to learn how to love me the way I feel loved."

These are just a few of the answers I've heard in the past two years when asking about a couple's reasons for resurfacing issues or separation.

When trying to explain the failure of modern marriage, most experts say we simply expect too much from matrimony.[1] They say we bring bloated hopes to the altar—that we inevitably find ourselves disappointed, and in our disillusionment we begin to feel like quitting. Thus, most marriage advice in one way or another revolves around learning to communicate these expectations and develop ways to get them mutually met over time.

In many ways, these experts are right. The common reasons for divorce cited above all seem to involve failed hopes. And it's certainly no secret that I—like many of us—brought unrealistic expectations to the altar.

Yet . . .

What has set me up for most of the unnecessary challenges in my marriage can't be explained by something as simple as heightened expectations. No, the real issue goes deeper than that. My issue, like for many today, is the mentality behind my expectations.

And unfortunately, it's not pretty.

ME-CENTRICITY.

The real epidemic is that our modern ideas of love lead us to, consciously or subconsciously, begin and end the conversation with what marriage can do for *me*. This has a way of taking a relationship designed for giving and making it all about getting. As a result, this me-centricity has a way of neutering the meaning and beauty of marriage altogether—which is, in fact, far bigger than any one of us.

ME-CENTRICITY THROUGHOUT HISTORY.

The Enlightenment and Self-Gratification. Some of the earlier roots of this me-centric brand of marriage can be seen throughout the era of history referred to as the Enlightenment, when the intellectuals of the eighteenth century attempted to advance society using reason and the scientific method. Previously, it was a generally accepted idea that the purpose of an individual's life was found in designated societal duties and a responsibility to the greater good. As new psychologies like individualism and self-gratification were popularized, many of the leading intellectuals began defining their purpose in life based on how fulfilled they were. This newly accepted self-fulfillment lens turned a spouse's approach to marriage on its head.[2]

It's the time in history when marriage quickly transitioned, as marriage law expert John Witte Jr. reflects, from a contract designed for "mutual love, procreation, and protection" to a contract designed for the "gratification of individual parties."[3] Furthermore, society began to view and value marriage as less about the good of another and the broader community, and more about an individual's emotional and sexual gratification.

Skip forward a few hundred years.

The American Revolution and Entitlement. "We hold these truths to be self-evident," reads the Declaration of Independence, "that all men are created equal, that they are endowed by their Creator with certain unalienable Rights, that among these are Life, Liberty and the pursuit of Happiness."[4]

On a societal level, these values have proved to be productive and—arguably—healthy. However, as they've seeped into our relational value systems, the narrative takes a turn. This perceived "right" to liberty and happiness permeating different layers of our lives can cultivate a paradigm in which everything in life subtly becomes about us. Many of us now live with this entitlement to personal liberties, independence, and the experience of happiness—often at the cost of more significant things in life. And sadly, this entitlement can easily misinform us about marriage.

It's not our inflated expectations that set us up for the severe disappointment that often leads to a broken marriage, though they certainly don't help. It's our entitlement. It's the bad idea that marriage is about me, and the cheap idea that I'm entitled to all the benefits of love without personal cost.

We walk the aisle, recite a few vows, and subconsciously expect marriage to be a genie in a bottle without a price tag—giving out endless happiness and breathtaking sex and ego massages all for free. Sadly, this me-centric entitlement has an intelligent way of killing our chances at the beautiful benefits marriage legitimately offers. And if we're ever going to discover these benefits, we've got to rethink our modern ideas about love itself.

GIVING, NOT GETTING.

Love happens to be one of the greater casualties of the English language. It's a blanket term we resort to for a variety of different feelings, attitudes, and emotions—ranging from affection to pleasure to deep attraction to common kindness. We love our favorite dessert. We love our brother. We love something insightful someone said today. We love having sex. We love being around people. We love smoking a cigar or drinking a glass of sweet tea.

In stark difference to English language's abuse of the word, ancient Hebrew seems to take better care of it.

Daniel Lapin, a Jewish businessman, tells a story about his former professor in his book *Thou Shall Prosper*. Apparently this particular prof used to tease his students by asking them before the Thanksgiving holiday if they liked turkey. He would then wait for the first student to innocently respond, "I love turkey," and then pounce. "No," he'd say. "You don't love turkey—if you did, you wouldn't eat it. You actually love yourself." He would then expand his analogy to relationships. If a young man tells a woman that he loves her when they are not married, the professor reasoned, his idea of love is just like that student who thinks he loves turkey. In reality, he simply loves himself.[5]

Lapin's professor was making light of our current misconceptions about love and setting them up to contrast to the meaning of love modeled by the Hebrew language. This Hebrew word for love— *ahava*—has little to do with what one feels or receives, as Lapin clarifies. To the contrary—*ahava* is actually a verb that means "I give."

This original paradigm of love is reflected when the apostle Paul says, "Husbands, go all out in your love for your wives, exactly as Christ did for the church—a love marked by giving, not getting."[6]

A love marked by giving and not getting creates ripples through our modern ideas about what love really is. As it turns out, love is not the fleeting butterflies we get when looking into the eyes of our significant other. It's not something we fall into when dating.

It's far simpler—and far wilder—than all that. To love another means to give.

This biblical brand of love finds its definition entirely outside of what we might get from it. On the contrary, this view of love includes all the everyday choices we make—big or small—to give to our spouse.

It's taking the trash out.

It's actively choosing to give him space when he is stressed.

It's a text message mid-afternoon to tell her you can't stop thinking about her.

It's the choice to not get triggered by something he said, but asking what he meant and how it makes him feel instead.

It's the time you're late for a meeting, but run back inside to tell your wife—who you know adores being told—how much she means to you that day.

It's the painful routine of taking the 3:00 a.m. newborn feeding shift so your wife can finally have three hours of uninterrupted sleep.

Love is not the twelve-part proposals or fairy-tale beginnings as much as it is the small, mundane but generous things we do for each other every day. Ann Voskamp, an author and refreshing voice on marriage, puts it perfectly when she says, "Real romance is really just sacrifice."[7] As we begin to orient ourselves to this incredible view of love that requires us to show up continually, we're sure to discover the beautiful paradox that it is.

LOVE IS BOTH/AND.

If we start and end with a me-centric mentality of what marriage can offer us, we miss the point of matrimony entirely. This biblical definition of love is a verb. It means work. It means sacrifice. And it makes marriage "both a gift," as German theologian Otto Piper says, "and a task to be accomplished."[8]

But before you hear me or anyone else say that marriage is *only* about your spouse, let's slow down.

While the me-centric mentality is damaging to marriage, the recently popular idea that marriage isn't about you is equally damaging. Though this selfless sentiment speaks in the right direction, it's not entirely accurate. Marriage is about you. In fact, this book is full of stories, studies, and principles to prove that it has incredible benefits to anyone willing to invest into it. Marriage is about you in the sense that it's about the betterment of *yourself*. It is about expressing yourself in giving to your spouse.

The real shift we must undertake is not as black and white as to whether marriage is about us or our spouse—about giving *or* getting—because all are universally true. The real shift is in the sequence with which we align these truths when approaching our marriages. Namely, our marriage is first about our spouse, then second about us. It's first about giving, and then about getting.

What's more, this sequence offers us a brand of love far better than any of its alternatives.

This original brand of love says, like Jesus does, that it is better to give than to receive.[9] And in doing so, it also implies that just because it's better to give than to receive does not mean that we won't receive at all. In fact, it's just the opposite. The Bible continually alludes to this paradox when it says that whatever a person sows, this he will also reap.[10]

THE MORE YOU GIVE TO MARRIAGE, THE MORE IT GIVES BACK.

Yes, marriage requires endless investment. But marriage is no cheapskate, either. The more we sow, the more we reap. The more we invest into it, the more return we see. The more we truly love, the more love gives back. (This is true even when our spouse fails to. For more on this see the section below, "Reciprocation Is Irrelevant.")

This is not about manipulating love to get what you want. This is about learning to genuinely love and give to your spouse and the brilliant effect it has on both of you.

Take a recent experiment I did in my own marriage as an example.

I spent the first few years of marriage with my version of the ever-popular me-centric and entitled mentality—expecting to reap where I hadn't sown. Then something Rabbi Shalom Arush wrote changed my perspective.

He wrote this of the reciprocal nature of love, "The gains that a spouse will feel on both a spiritual and material level defy description, once they make loving their spouse first place."[11]

I questioned the validity of his statement at first, but the concept intrigued me. So I put the scientific method to good use. It was as simple as this. (For graphics and more details on this experiment and its results, see "Cave Talk.")

Part One: For thirty-one days, I attempted to do five things every day to intentionally love my wife and communicate she is the most important thing to me.

Part Two: I then rated my performance and measured my experience in five different areas of my life on a scale from one to ten every night before I went to bed. Those five areas included our general quality of life, peace in the home, marital enjoyment, career productivity, and children's behavior.

To my surprise, thirty-one days later, I had a chart of data and an arsenal of experiences proving that intentionally loving my wife does, in fact, change every other layer of my life.

On the days I intentionally attempted to give to my wife, the benefits were obnoxiously clear by the numbers on my chart. I was happier and more hopeful. My stress and negativity considerably decreased. We experienced more peace in our home—with fewer fights and meltdowns and less complaining. My wife and I wanted to be around each other more and enjoyed each other's company. My time at work was more focused and productive. Even my one-year-old son's behavior was noticeably better—judging by fewer meltdowns or tantrums.

More specifically, my marriage made the shift . . .

From nights on the couch to expedited conflict. Prior to the last thirty-one days, it was a weekly occurrence for my wife and me to let our tempers escalate to a level ten and then stubbornly make them remain there for some time. Yet I soon realized that if my wife felt loved, our conflict level rarely hit an eight. Even when the tempers did flare, the time we allowed them to hang around dramatically decreased.

From rants to enjoying the moments. For the most part of the previous year, every time my wife finally got my attention she often had so much pent-up frustration that we spent the little time we had together working through that comment I made six days ago. Over these thirty-one days, however, we both learned to enjoy our time together rather than treating it as an opportunity to air our frustrations. I noticed that Analee was quicker to let things go and not keep track of my relational deficiencies. As a result of her graciousness in this area, I found myself eager to spend time with her—and she felt the same way about me.

From needy self-entitlement to the empowerment of each other. Previously, when my wife's basic emotional needs weren't consistently being met, she was far more inclined to pull me away from things that I loved—the things that refueled me. This typically backfired, because it created a cycle in which Analee needed me in fifth gear just as I needed more gas in the tank. However, as I used these thirty-one days to intentionally give to my wife, I began witnessing in her the most bizarre behavior. She started asking if I wanted to watch football or grab a cigar with the boys. It was as if the more important she felt in my eyes, the more she championed the things that allowed me to relax or come alive.

From competing to contributing. Like most entrepreneurs, I thrive in productivity and the challenge of juggling many moving pieces all at once. During these thirty-one days, my marriage—and its conflict—transformed from the greatest resistance to my productivity at work to one of my career's most valuable assets. On the days my wife felt genuinely valued, she advocated for me to invest deeply in my work. It was as if she stopped competing with my career for my attention, and instead joined my team to partner in my career with me. I soon found that my wife's championing of me in my career pursuits has been the most professionally empowering experience I'd ever had.

My experiment provides simply one example that Jesus and the rabbi were on to something. Specifically, it would seem that it is, in fact, better to give than to simply expect to receive in marriage. Because when we do learn to love well by investing ourselves deeply, we can expect marriage to come with extraordinary benefits. Even more than that, we can expect marriage to become our greatest asset in life.

However, as most of us are already aware, there's a big difference between knowing what real love is and actually loving. One takes a cognitive assent. The other takes everyday choices. In the never-ending wrestle to put real love into practice, the central question becomes "*How*?"

Glad you asked.

GIVING vs INTELLIGENT GIVING

Early on in our marriage, I was convinced that my wife had a bottomless love tank, as Dr. Gary Chapman has written about in *The 5 Love Languages*. At the very least, it seemed broken and leaky because I could never seem to fill it sufficiently. The more I gave to marriage, the more it asked of me—making it feel impossible to ever get ahead. My wife constantly felt unloved and I felt perpetually exhausted. Clearly something had to change.

Upon closer examination, my wife's love tank wasn't broken, nor was it bottomless. As it turns out, most assets in our lives will inevitably become a liability if not intelligently maintained. This is true for our car, our bank account, and it is certainly true for our marriages. Though I prided myself on investing efficiently in my day job, I was apparently insanely inefficient at home.

How? Because investment is thoroughly useless unless applied to the right things.

Motivated by exhaustion, I began investigating the difference between giving and intelligent giving. My exploration led me to three ideas.

Allow me to introduce you to them.

1. Marriage is designed for first place

I like to call this the "Priority Phenomenon," which you can see at work in my home experiment. Simply put, outside of a relationship with the Divine, marriage is designed to be given first place in our life priorities. More so, the phenomenon implies that *where* marriage falls in the sequence of our priorities is more important than the *amount of* time, energy, and resources we give to it.

This means that we can invest endless amounts of time and love into our spouse—but the moment they feel less important than our work, or friends, or hobbies, our efforts of love will cease to be enough.

Once the sequence of our priorities is properly in place and we're ready to invest, a mathematical equation can become incredibly helpful.

2. 80 percent of the output comes from 20 percent of the input

Also known as the 80/20 rule, the Pareto principle was drawn from the observation of an early twentieth century economist. After observing various patterns in life such as wealth distribution, the growth of vegetables, and the general amount of investment required in various professions, Vilfredo Pareto concluded that in virtually every area of life, we can trace 20 percent of our input to 80 percent of its output (and vice versa). Here are a few examples to make sense of it.[12]

- 80% (or more) of the results come from 20% (or less) of the effort and time invested.
- 80% of revenue comes from 20% of the client base.
- 80% of the health of our marriage is cultivated by 20% of our investment.

The beauty of Pareto's principle is that if you can identify that 20 percent and focus on it, you can save yourself from expending un-necessary—and unhelpful—time, energy, and investment in your marriage. Though we know there are no real universal formulas to having a successful marriage, the 80/20 principle can serve as a helpful guide to putting your days of exhaustion without fulfill-ment behind you.

But the first question here is perhaps the hardest one. "What is the 20 percent in your relationship?" And the answer lies in the truth that . . .

3. Everyone speaks a different language

I could make every effort to spend time with my wife, hold her hand, kiss her—but if I don't understand her love language, I still may find myself at the end of the day saying good night to a woman who does not feel loved.

Dr. Gary Chapman, of course, popularized this idea in his landmark book, *The 5 Love Languages*. As Dr. Chapman told me, "If you're not speaking your spouse's love language, it doesn't matter how much you're giving, you will never answer her deepest questions about your love or fill her love tank completely."

You can design the best investment plan possible for your spouse—but unless you know how he or she truly receives love, your efforts are destined for little more than a heartless "nice try." On the other hand, if you can identify exactly what is required to make your spouse feel loved, you'll be well on your way to identifying that 20 percent that can make all the difference.

If the love language idea is new to you, take ten minutes right now and take the free *5 Love Languages* inventory: 5lovelanguages.com/

profile. Trust me—it's guaranteed to save you a lot of time in the future.

Analee's Point of View. *Understanding our love languages changed everything for us. Do it! I was certain that I was loving Tyler to the max. How could he not be overwhelmed with all my loving? I was verbally affirming, went out of my way to do things for him—always thinking of ways to bless him. But words had little significance to him and it didn't matter much if I did acts of service. I learned that it meant everything to him when I would stop dancing around singing affirmations, and instead simply be still with him, cuddle, and spend quality time in deep conversation.*

RECIPROCATION IS IRRELEVANT
How to Respond When Your
Spouse Doesn't Seem to Care

"What if I give and give and give, but my spouse doesn't reciprocate?" Since publishing thoughts on the priority phenomenon, this is the dominant question I've received in response. So I've asked every marriage expert I could. Their answers are varied and enlightening.

LOVE STIMULATES LOVE.

"Love is a choice," Dr. Gary Chapman told me when I had the chance to spend an hour interviewing him. "We can request love, but we cannot demand love. We cannot make our spouse speak our love language. However, my basic approach is that you can't control your spouse but you can control your attitude and your behavior."

He continued, "The good news is that love stimulates love. And though the object of love is not getting something you want but doing something for the well-being of the one you love, it is a fact that when we receive love we are far more likely to be motivated to reciprocate and do something our spouse desires."

When I asked him for a practical suggestion on how to get started, he said, "Try this: Choose an attitude of love. Learn the love language of your spouse and speak it on a regular basis. Then three months down the road you can say to them, 'On a scale of zero to ten, how much love do you feel coming from me?' If they give you a seven, eight, nine, ten—you're at the top. Or if they say anything less than ten, you say, 'What can I do to bring it up to a ten or bring it up to a nine?' and they give you a suggestion, then to the best of your ability you do that."

Dr. Chapman recommended repeating this process every two weeks by simply asking your spouse what you can do to love them better, and taking their answer to heart.

"There's a good chance that before long they're going to say, 'Well, wait a minute here. I'm turning this around. On a scale of zero to ten, how much love do you feel coming from me?'"[13]

And that is exactly how love stimulates love.

THE SCHOOL OF LOVE.

Gary Thomas, author of *Sacred Marriage*, shared some great insight on the issue in a recent interview with me as well.

He started by paraphrasing Luke 6 in which Jesus says, " 'If you love those that love you, what good is that to you? If you give to receive, what good is that? Even the world loves that way. If you're kind to those that are kind to you, well that's how the world operates. How does that prove it there? Jesus loves even your enemies, do good to them.' Then He says, 'And men, love them without expecting to get anything back.' "

Gary continued, "God doesn't command us to get married; He offers it to us as an opportunity. God lets us choose whom we're going to love. Yes, this spouse might be difficult to love at times, but that's what marriage is for—to teach us how to love. And once I accept that my greatest need is to learn how to love—not to be loved—then the things that used to frustrate me about my marriage, now I appreciate . . . There isn't a day when marriage doesn't give you an opportunity to love."

I love Gary's idea here of marriage as the best school for learning love—in which, as he says, the very "things that tick us off become training." He explained to me, "I need to learn how to love somebody who's impatient . . . I might need to learn to love somebody who is selfish. My marriage gives me an opportunity to do that."

So what does this look like practically, I asked Gary. Here's his response: "Allow your marriage relationship to stretch your love and to enlarge your capacity for love. Use marriage as a practice court, where you learn to accept another person and serve him or her. And please don't limit this love to 'spiritual' things like praying, preaching, and exhorting. Part of the experience of love is delighting each other in very earthy ways."[14]

Logically, it doesn't make sense to me that it is better to give than to receive. But practically, this theory seems to work in marriage. If I'm focusing on giving to my wife, I experience great joy. This joy is connected to my worship because I'm loving my wife out of love for my heavenly Father.

On the other hand, if I'm in my marriage only to receive, there's a lust released in me. Suddenly, I can't be loved enough. I can't be appreciated enough. I can't be paid attention to enough. And so I think Jesus is just telling us, "You get to choose where your marriage is headed. Are you in this together only to receive love, or to learn how to love?"

It's up to us. But I think we all know where the greatest joy is.

CHAPTER FOUR

ONE + ONE = ONE

Love Isn't Something We Fall Into

> *"A successful marriage requires falling in love many times, always with the same person."*
> *—Mignon McLaughlin*

I'll never forget the first time I said "I love you" to Analee. It was an absolute nightmare.

Some people find it incredibly easy to start professing their love for a significant other. Then there's me. Up until this point in life, I was able to avoid using the infamous three words and had no intention of dusting them off until marriage. Of course, that was before I met the five-foot-nothing firecracker I now call my wife.

It was a lazy late afternoon in Los Angeles and two influencing dynamics were in play.

First, Analee and I had just hit the six-month-dating mark—a big deal among twentysomethings—and we had made a unanimous decision to keep this exclusive experiment going. This newfound mutual commitment was like pouring gasoline on an already raging fire, which had a way of extending our lip-locking sessions and inspiring more and more time together.

Second, though we both were aware of each other's spirituality, we had not yet shared many of our thoughts about God. Even if you go to the same church or gathering, often your thoughts about the character of God can greatly differ, having dramatic implications on the way you want to design your relationship and family and life. This conversation was a massive missing piece of our relationship's puzzle.

We had recently braved this "thoughts on God" conversation and the shared perspective we found calmed any possible doubt about developing a future together. To make our newfound connection even hotter, she had just mentioned that she was halfway through a book written by one of my favorite spiritual thinkers. I asked her to read a chapter or two as we spent our afternoon together.

Analee diligently read aloud in her best narrator's voice, but the only voice I was listening to was the one in my head telling me that I had found the one I was looking for.

Then it just happened.

Before she could even finish the sentence—and about as awkwardly as you could imagine—I cut her off.

"I love you."

Analee's Point of View. *I was thinking, Am I boring him or is he just not interested in the chapter? Then out of nowhere— with no warning or tact—he blurted out those three words. I didn't know what to think. I knew he had never said those words to any- one before and part of me was obviously ecstatic to hear it. But the other part of me was like, "Now?! Sitting on my couch while reading a book? You just waited your whole life to say those three words and you couldn't even wait for me to finish my sentence?! Or perhaps a more romantic, special setting?! What do I do? Do*

I say it back?" Oh, gosh. I tried really hard to hide my smile, but couldn't stop nervously giggling.

She had stopped reading, though her eyes never left the book. I wasn't sure if it was the daunting words that made her uncomfortable, or just the general awkwardness of a guy cutting her off to randomly profess his love. Or worse, maybe both. Either way, she was obviously stunned speechless.

I panicked. Then my thoughts crucified me.

How could I wait my entire life to say this to a woman and let it go down like this?

On a random Sunday afternoon?!

We've only been dating for six months!

I couldn't even wait for her to finish her sentence?!

Do I even really love her? Or am I just being impulsive?

Am I ready for this?

No. We're not ready for this yet.

I've blown it!

Still, she sat silently. And in a matter of seconds, my mind rocketed from confidence to fear to intimidation to regret to rational reasoning—but all emotions in the end pointed to one thing: *This was a colossal mistake.*

So, I did what any relational moron would do in this situation . . .

"I'm sorry. We aren't ready for this. Can I take it back?"

Analee's Point of View. *"WHAT?! Who does that? I felt like we were in fifth grade. You just told me you loved me for the first time in your life and now you're taking it back?!"*

I could already tell by the look on her face that it was too late.

"Of course you can take it back." She said with a smirk, "But I already know the truth."

Analee's Point of View. *And the truth will set you free!*

It's only one of the epic blunders I made while dating my wife that we still laugh about today. However, my pathetic delivery is only half the humor in the story. The arguably more humorous part is that I actually believed that what we were experiencing in that season was falling "*in love.*"

Turns out, I wasn't "*in love*" with my wife at all. Not then. Not on our wedding day. And in some moments, not even now.

Analee's Point of View. *For all the rest of you hopeless romantics out there like me, just hold on. It's only wordplay! And you're about to find out exactly what it means.*

LOVE IS A VICTIM OF MODERN CULTURE.

It's a classic conclusion: "I think we're falling in love." At some point, you gather the courage to see if the sentiment is reciprocated, then, of course, you start talking long-term. And why wouldn't you talk marriage? After all, love is the foundation for marriage, right?

This was certainly my story. After a few stomach butterflies, a few DTRs (Define the Relationship), and plenty of time together, I thought Analee and I had arrived at the much-sought-after phenomenon of being in love.

Unfortunately for us and our socially reinforced illusions, love isn't something we simply fall into.

However, infatuation is.

INFATUATION vs LOVE.

First, the bad news.

We often assume the emotions we feel in dating and the early stage of marriage are evidence of love. However, these emotions are better explained by the consistent neurochemical reaction that biology calls the state of infatuation.[1]

The early stage of romantic attraction and a cocaine high may have drastically different effects on a person's life, but both endeavors share quite a bit in common. Each one induces a rush of several chemicals to your brain. One of the more dominant of these chemicals is called dopamine—otherwise known as our body's reward drug. This means that when our brain tastes the chemical, it instantly dispenses a reward of positive emotions throughout our body. As Helen Fisher, an anthropologist at Rutgers University reflects, "The properties of infatuation have many of the same elements of a cocaine high. Most importantly, infatuation can overtake the rational part of your brain."[2]

Now, let's not take the association of infatuation and cocaine too far. Obviously experiencing a heightened rush of dopamine is not inherently a negative thing. In fact, it is a completely natural and healthy and celebrated part of romance. Even when the Bible walks us through the stages of an epic love story between Solomon and his Shulamite bride, infatuation plays a foundational role both in the beginning and all throughout their relationship. Song of Solomon reads, "Kiss me—full on the mouth! Yes! For your love is better than wine . . . Take me away with you! Let's run off together!

An elopement with my King-Lover! We'll celebrate, we'll sing, we'll make great music. Yes! For your love is better than vintage wine. Everyone loves you—of course! And why not?"[3]

Analee's Point of View. *Whatever you want to call it, I love infatuation! I am so thankful God lets us have the love-drug high and I don't believe it's off-limits throughout marriage. I sing "So-ber" by Little Big Town often as I dance around my kitchen: "'Cause I love being in love. It's the best kind of drug . . ."*

Infatuation doesn't lack virtue or purpose. It is a beautiful and powerful dynamic in a relationship. However, it's our modern tendency to confuse this chemical reaction with being in love that can be damaging to our marriages.

Why? To begin, science has proven that the intensity of this neurochemical reaction doesn't typically last longer than twenty-four months at a time.[4] This "in-love" sensation ebbs and flows throughout a relationship. In the early stages, it fills a deep emotional need to be cared for and appreciated by another. But in time, the intensity of this chemical "high" inevitably fades.

The damage ensues when we closely associate this important but short-lived season of infatuation with true love—only to find ourselves two weeks, one year, or three anniversaries into marriage without the same butterflies we once felt. The trap is when we're left to assume, as many have, that somewhere along the way we've fallen *out* of love, and perhaps are left questioning if our love was ever real in the first place.

By mistaking infatuation for real love, we've equated the defining reality of marriage as little more than an emotion we can take a hit of to get a twelve to eighteen month high. And somehow we still act shocked when 50 percent of people leave their relationships as the feelings fade in search of the next fix.[5]

We'll take a closer look at this shortly, but let's be clear. Our common understanding of being "in love" is often not the kind of "love" marriage was designed for.

The good news? The brand of love marriage was designed for is far better than being drunk on dopamine.

LOVE IS A JOURNEY—NOT A FREE FALL.

As products of an instantly gratified society, we are increasingly drawn to microwaving everything in life. We prefer our hamburger drive-thrus and our personalized Netflix queues. As we discussed in the last chapter, many of us come into marriage with a sense of entitlement, wanting what we want from this relationship for free. But there's another common misconception many of us come strapped with to the altar. We tend to expect the benefits of marriage instantly as well.

But expecting everything at the click of a button hasn't set us up well for true love.

I'll be the first to admit that I brought this microwave mentality into marriage. It wasn't that my motivations were wrong. I wanted a real companionship—fully loaded with emotional support—a safe and trusted friendship, and breathtaking sex. And as social research has shown us, all of these things are very real benefits of marriage.[6] Where I went wrong is that I subconsciously expected all these benefits on day one.

Anyone who has experienced marriage knows that true companionship comes from years of conversation. A real emotional connection requires trust-building circumstances over time. And breathtaking sex? Well, it can take time to learn each other physically too.

Analee's Point of View. *I definitely had a few of these misconceptions coming into marriage. However, most of them were things that I assumed without realizing it. I assumed that easy capizzi would be the way of life for us. I assumed that Ty and I would have meaningful connected conversations all the time—the kind of oneness where the other person felt so safe and alive because we could practically read each other's minds. Ha! Wrong-o!*

Unfortunately, a microwave mentality seems to be a dime-a-dozen in modern marriages and is only perpetuated by the previously mentioned illusion of falling "in love" with our spouse. Our marital responsibilities then subtly become about little more than maintaining this state of love—and we've all seen where this rabbit hole can lead.

Inevitably the challenges of marriage come knocking, and because we think we've already "arrived" in love, any level of conflict can have a way of putting this love on trial.

Fortunately, this instant brand of love that you simply fall into is not what God had in mind when creating man and woman.

Gary Thomas spoke brilliantly about this when I interviewed him. "A good marriage isn't something you find and fall into," he said. "It's something you make and remake many times over. See, in the Hollywood view of 'falling in love,' it's all about finding the right person and then it's supposed to be easy. Unfortunately, this idea ignores the fact that we become different people. It ignores the fact that we usually want different things out of life. It ignores the fact that really, about 80 percent of us are going to marry almost our exact opposite. It assumes that we're static individuals and we're not. Life changes. People get sick. Their parents die—that changes us. They get cancer—that changes us. They get fired— that changes us. They might succeed in their business far more than they imagined—that changes us. If we don't pursue intimacy, we lose intimacy. I have to keep pursuing my wife or I'll become a stranger to my wife."[7]

So knowing all this, I asked, how can a person choose a spouse wisely or marry well? I loved Gary's answer: "Marriage is not about finding 'the One' and falling in love. It's about choosing one and, over time, *becoming* the 'right couple'.'"

Perhaps we can internalize this idea a bit better if we change our language—starting with this idea of oneness.

BECOMING ONE.

The Bible never seems to mention the idea of "falling in love." It does talk, however, about the process of "becoming one." It says (emphasis mine), "A man [*leaves*] his father and his mother, and shall *cleave* unto his wife: and they shall *be one* flesh."[8] As practical as this seems, many scholars believe that this process of becoming one is far more than a wedding, moving in together, and merging bank accounts. The reference actually speaks to a spiritual, emotional, and material journey of two people learning how to love each other and integrate their lives together. As we look closer, we'll find that this simple verse happens to capture a beautiful picture of a marriage worth fighting for.

Throughout history, many have studied this journey of two becoming one. My favorite take on this comes from Mary Anne McPherson Oliver in her book *Conjugal Spirituality*. She explains, "The joint life of a couple [is built] throughout three stages that aren't strictly chronological, but are ongoing and alternating aspects of [two becoming one]."[9] Let's take a look at the different stages.

1. The Leaving Stage: Creating a New Reality

British novelist and fellow Inklings member Charles Williams calls this early stage of marriage "a mutual invasion, where both selves are broken down so they can be transformed by the love they both receive."[10] Emile Durkheim, the father of modern sociology, suggests similarly that this stage is "a dramatic act, in which two strangers come together and match differing definitions of reality."[11]

Most people associate this stage of "leaving" with the departure from one's family of origin in order to begin a new family. This is certainly part of the leaving stage, but only the beginning.

The initial stage of marriage—that can last up to fourteen years— is entirely about learning how to merge two separate realities to create a new one, both internally and externally.[12] And this means more than changing last names and zip codes. Throughout these years, every aspect of each individual's reality will be reevaluated.

There's no question that this is the most unnatural and challenging stage of becoming one. The forming of a new reality means letting go of our former one—whether we want to or not. This process requires both parties developing the maturity over time to negotiate a reality that both are excited to live in.

Even on a basic biological level, it takes the brain ten to fifteen years to change its previously developed neurological tracks or patterns of thinking.[13] This process, called neuroplasticity, helps explain why the first few years of becoming one can feel incredibly unnatural. Sadly, many of those who choose to divorce in this stage don't actually give themselves a chance to experience the real payoff in marriage.

This season of leaving requires that we learn—through trial and error—how to communicate with one another and channel the long-forgotten virtue of patience.[14] However, such patience is not without payoff. In the midst of this wrestling into a new reality, we are given a beautiful hope: if we stay loyal to the everyday choices to love our spouse, we can create a culture, a new reality, in our marriages where the wild benefits of true love do exist.

2. The Cleaving Stage: Life as Partnership

Life is scientifically defined as the ability to produce new cells, but it is just as important to structure those cells inside a functional system.[15] This second season of marriage is all about focusing this new reality and the discoveries of the leaving season to optimize a couple's partnership in life together.

"Renunciation and creation are supplemented by the courage to continue widening the self, the curious probing to understand the spark of Divinity in the other, and patient prioritizing to maintain the equilibrium which has been achieved,"[16] Oliver says. In other words, this season is all about using life to grow closer and using your closeness to succeed in life.

This involves learning how to keep a connection with one another while incorporating and harmonizing the daily rhythms of each other's career, family, and life responsibilities. Because of this season's demand for perseverance and diligence, couples can find themselves disconnected during these years if they don't remain intentional.

A conversation I recently had with Ray Ortlund, a brilliant pastor and a husband married for over forty years, seems to capture the virtue of this stage of marriage well.

"My wife was given to me to enrich me," he said, "to make me wiser, a better man, a better professional, and a better father . . .

Once I stopped being so stubborn and learned to use our relationship and her voice as the asset that it is, everything changed."[17]

According to Ray, as well as many sociological studies, the payoffs in this season are spiritual, relational, sociological, and economic.

3. The Oneness Stage: A Celebration

The road to oneness is long and not always easy, but the outcome is something to be celebrated. Oliver explains, "As two mature individuals turn obstacles into trampolines and continue in mutual conquest and surrender, an easy and real creative union of mind, body and heart will take place."[18]

"As love grows older," says Chinese-American "Artist of Life" Bruce Lee, "our hearts mature and our love becomes as coals, deep-burning and unquenchable." In this season, couples enjoy "comfortable companionship and mutual affirmation," as Oliver describes it.[19]

The Bible also offers another portrait of oneness worth celebrating. In the context of the Trinity—the Father, Son, and Holy Spirit—oneness simply means living in perpetual celebration of one another. This is the goal of marriage as well. Imagine a lifestyle of deep celebration of each other—despite both of your dysfunction, wounds, and blind spots.

It is within this celebration of one another that our greatest human potential emerges. In the presence of this kind of love, we're given the chance to become the best versions of ourselves for the world.

MICROWAVES ARE FOR DINNERS.

This journey into oneness speaks to a simple idea that dramatically confronts our modern instant brand of love. The beautiful truth is that Analee and I weren't celebrating our arrival into love on our wedding day. We were simply—and profoundly—committing to a lifelong journey to become one by choosing to love each other.

Being "in love" isn't an *instant* destination we find while dating. Love isn't something we happen to stumble into—it's far more active and powerful than that. Being "in love" is a new reality of oneness in our marriages formed through a pilgrimage of everyday choices to put each other first. Such a dramatic new reality takes time, diligence, and plenty of patience to create.

But then again, that's a relational reality worth fighting for.

My friend Jared Black recently told me a story that captures the problem with a microwave marriage.[20]

He and his wife, Stephanie, were visiting with a group of new friends. In their introductions, Jared casually mentioned that he and Stephanie had been married for five years. Without missing a beat, one woman shot back in her Southern drawl, "Five years of marriage? It's like y'all are in kindergarten!"

It was an awkward comment, but the truth behind it deeply impacted Jared's perspective. In retelling the story to me, he reflected, "Until that moment, I had never considered marriage—our marriage—through the lens of a developmental cycle. I guess I had somehow just assumed that marriage was an event that happened on a specific date, in a specific year. As far as I was concerned, I was married . . . end of story. However, the thought of a kindergartener—full of potential, full of questions, and a developing future, not to mention all the tantrums, immaturity, and poor communication—seemed to be a better description of what my wife and I had been experiencing from day to day."

According to Jared, this simple offhand comment put his first four years of marriage into clearer focus. Of course he and Stephanie struggled to communicate and make decisions together—they were just beginners at this crazy thing called marriage!

Jared continued, "Being able to view our marriage during those times as if we were, say, a three-year-old child helped ease the pressure of supposedly knowing how to be married. A three-year-old can't be expected to act and communicate like an adult. So why would we, a newly married, three-year-old couple know any better?"

His story was liberating to Analee and me as well, allowing us some extra grace for the "leaving" stage of our marriage that we are currently navigating. Yes, the hope for a kindergartener is to grow out of the immaturity of vying for attention, temper tantrums, and selfishness, to become a fully functioning, mature, capable adult. But that doesn't mean we expect them to act like an adult today, either.

I love how Jared described this tension: "Marriage isn't something we accomplished the day we said 'I do.' It is an ongoing action discovered with our spouses—a development cycle. The day of marriage simply creates a brand-new infant couple, pledging to learn the art of marrying their individual lives into one combined, maturing life together."

As Jared suggests, let's abandon our microwave mentalities. Let's give our marriages (and spouses) a break—since we know we're all still three-year-olds throwing tantrums and barely able to dress ourselves. Instead of demanding all the promised perks of marriage today, let's consider that oneness is a beautiful, but long journey together.

Now for the practical. Here are a few suggestions I've found helpful in curbing my tendency to microwave my marriage.

LEARN THE ART OF CONVERSATION

*"A happy marriage is a long conversation
that always seems too short."*
—Andre Maurois

Ray and Jani Ortlund have been married for forty-two years. As I sat across a burger and a sweet tea from Ray, I asked what his favorite thing about their marriage was now, as opposed to the first thirty years. His answer was beautiful: "Our relationship is one constant and flowing conversation where no walls or inhibitions exist."

In a society where an "inability to communicate" is commonly cited as a reason of divorce, conversation with your spouse is a lost art.

Yet, according to most experts, the early stages of marriage are built on a couple's ability to communicate and relate to one another—verbally and nonverbally.[21] "And even when talk may seem like the most natural thing in the world," Mary Anne McPherson Oliver says, "using it to create long-lasting intimacy is not natural or simple . . . The couple must develop skills."[22]

Analee and I are right in the middle of learning this art of conversation together. And though the art of conversation has not come easy for us, there have been a few invaluable best practices we've come across—each one having proved well worth experimenting with.

1. Drive-thru conversations

"Being listened to," as Mennonite pastor David Augsburger says, "is so close to being loved that most people cannot tell the difference."[23] Yet more often than not, listening is more an act of waiting for our chance to be heard. This can keep us running in circles while talking "at" our spouse and not landing anywhere by talking "with" them.

In his book *Making Love Last Forever*, Gary Smalley introduces an exercise called drive-thru conversations that has helped Analee and me significantly.[24] It goes like this.

Spouse #1 shares his or her mind. Once the appropriate time comes for Spouse #2 to respond, Spouse #2 paraphrases what Spouse #1 has just said, gives Spouse #1 the chance to confirm or correct, then finally, Spouse #2 responds.

This simple tool has several layers. It demands that both parties actively listen, which keeps them from being too quick to speak. It also leaves little room for applying your own assumptions to your spouse's words and so triggering a misunderstanding. But perhaps most valuable is the way it slows a conversation to a pace where you're more likely to actually hear what your spouse is saying and less likely to butt in with something you're guaranteed to regret.

2. Write a new language

Often couples enter marriage with two radically different vocabularies. A word or gesture that means one thing to one of you might carry an entirely different connotation for the other.

Analee and I decided that one of the better uses of our funds early in marriage would be to consistently go to marriage counseling throughout our first few years together. Counseling gave us a lot of priceless tools for our relationship, none more valuable than a common language to avoid many of the emotional mishaps that so often get lost in translation.

Analee's Point of View. *If I could say one thing to newlyweds or people who are interested in improving their marriage, it would be to invest in counseling or inner healing as a couple. We have so many hurts from childhood and past relationships that we don't even realize alter our actions and reactions—and hinder our vulnerability and the giving and receiving of love. Our commitment to going to counseling every two weeks in the first year of marriage was the best thing we spent our time and money on. The other thing that radically changed our relationship when things were hard was an inner-healing week called Restoring the Foundations. We spent a week discovering wounds in our hearts that were holding us back, learning to forgive each other and ourselves, and recommitting our promise to love each other well and maintain a healthy heart. We still, to this day, revisit the lessons we learned and materials we got there. Priceless!*

Even if you don't have the money or interest to go to counseling, you might read marriage books together or simply make it a habit to ask, "What did you mean by that?" Regardless of how you write this new language, one thing is for sure: if you are proactive about it, you will save yourself an incredible amount of time and emotional energy that would otherwise be wasted by misunderstanding each other.

3. Sit down

The mid-century French developed a set of practices for marriage. One of these practices is called *le devoir de s'asseoir*, directly translated as "the duty to sit down."[25] They believed that simply scheduling time to have conversations together could change the landscape of a marriage.

I think anyone who has experienced the effects of intentionally and consistently connecting via conversation with your spouse would agree that it does indeed change everything.

You may want to get your iCals out now.

In the end, you have to find what works for you. But consider yourself warned. Many older and wiser than I have claimed that the long-term health of a marriage lives and dies on a couple's ability to converse.

SECRETS DON'T MAKE MARRIAGES

How to Cultivate Emotional Intimacy

Do you have to talk about *everything*? Is keeping secrets from your spouse ever okay? Or are secrets always unhelpful to becoming one?

The issue of secrets in marriage is one of the more divided conversations among marriage counselors today. One camp finds it acceptable, depending on the circumstance and emotional framework of the partners. Others find the very thought of secret-keeping appalling. And though my experience with Analee speaks in strong support of one of these camps, I thought I'd invite a few people far more experienced than I into the conversation.

Lori and Barry Byrne, authors of *Love After Marriage*, were kind enough to agree to an interview with me, and in our time together, I asked them about secret-keeping in marriage.[26]

Their suggestion? To first take one big step backward. "It's not as much about keeping secrets or not keeping secrets as it is about knowing and being known." Clarifying something I had read in their book, they went on to say, "Knowing and being known is not only fundamental to all of humanity, but it's the most basic foundation of real, intimate relationship. And healthy intimacy exists between two people who both know and are known by each other in a deep, personal way."[27]

As I inquired more about this, three suggestions of how to cultivate this healthy intimacy seemed to emerge.

1. Clean out your closet

We'll come back to my time with Lori and Barry.

I want to invite one of my favorite people into the conversation. You may know William Paul Young as the author of *The Shack*. Analee and I know him as the officiant of our wedding. He also happens to be the perfect person to talk to about the significance of secrets in marriage. Over fifteen years ago now, Paul spent four days telling his wife all of his secrets.

"It took me four full days to destroy all my facades and everything she thought she knew and trusted. I hit the bottom and there was nothing pretty about it."[28]

I asked him why refusing to have secrets is so important in a marriage, and his response was beautiful: "Can you imagine the Father, Son, and Holy Spirit keeping a hidden life from each other? Love itself is implicitly grounded in knowing. Trust is built around knowing and secrets are always un-knowings. Leanne Payne wrote, 'The unconfessed is the unhealed.' You cannot keep secrets compartmentalized in your inside house away from life and relationships. They will pollute even those things that are true and right and beautiful, staining them with its own darkness until one can no longer distinguish between the 'real' and the 'presented.' Sadly, we—and our marriages—will continue to be as sick as the secrets we keep."

The Byrnes put it simply: "As George MacDonald says, 'Few delights can equal the mere presence of the one whom we trust utterly.' And you cannot trust utterly when secrets exist between you."

2. Keep an open conversation and practice forgiveness

As Lori and Barry write in *Love After Marriage*, "While it is true that you can learn a lot by observing, real intimacy requires that you talk openly about your personal thoughts and feelings. It is only by talking openly and honestly that you can really work together on issues that affect your marriage and confirm what you think you know about your spouse."[29]

And forgiveness? Yes, it's easier said than done. But if we are ever going to develop real intimacy with our spouse, we must become a safe place for them. We must learn how to openly accept their attempts to be honest, open, and vulnerable. And we must learn how to genuinely forgive them when their secrets hurt us. If they are brave enough to open the conversation, don't cut it short—practice forgiveness, and keep the conversation going.

3. Don't forget to love yourself

"If you don't like the gift you're giving," Lori says, "you're not going to give it freely."

In *Love After Marriage*, Barry elaborates, "The final step in cultivating intimacy is learning to live in such a way that we will feel good about ourselves before God."[30] The truth is that if we feel guilt about something we're doing or shame in who we are, we won't ever get vulnerable with anyone. Shame and guilt want to keep things hidden. But when we learn to accept and love ourselves, living openly and intimately with others becomes far more natural.

This self-love is counterintuitively a key to a successful modern marriage. We find its basis in the nuance of Jesus' second greatest ask of us. In Matthew 22:39, He says, "You shall love your neighbor as yourself." The implication here is that we must first love ourselves to genuinely love another person.

NEVER STOP EXPLORING

Why You Will Never Fully Know Your Spouse

Jonathan Jackson is an actor (currently playing Avery Barkley in *Nashville*), musician and songwriter, writer, poet, husband, father, and a close friend. He also happens to be an Eastern Orthodox Christian with some refreshing perspectives on life.

Today we tend to bring a destination mentality into marriage. As we've discussed, we fall "in love" while dating and then celebrate our arrival into this love on our wedding day. Our marital life then becomes about little more than maintaining this state, rather than progressively growing in intimacy.

In my opinion, this destination mentality kills marriages—though I'm not exempt from it myself. So in an attempt to change my own mind and see loving my wife as a journey of continual exploration, I landed in a conversation with Jonathan about the Orthodox belief of Apophatic theology.

I know, it's a big word—so I'll let Jonathan explain.[31]

Jonathan, you've mentioned how healthy it is to avoid thinking you fully know someone and to keep a level of mystery in any relationship. Does this thread of thought come from anywhere in particular?

"It does, but I'll have to give you a quick history lesson to explain.

"Over the centuries and particularly after the Great Schism in 1054, Western Christianity became more and more scholastic in nature. It embraced systematic theology and rationalism and slowly developed away from what many call 'the mystery of faith.'

"The Orthodox Church [historically identified as Eastern Christianity], on the other hand, maintained this element of faith, more specifically, known as Apophatic theology. This essentially means that man cannot ever fully know God and especially not through rationalism or abstract study alone. But by humbly professing what we cannot know about God, it places the human heart in an atmosphere capable of encountering God experientially, as opposed to intellectually or theoretically. In essence, man and woman will spend eternity growing closer to God, but never exhausting the mystery."

So what does this belief have to do with marriage?

"Every human is created in the image of God. We see throughout Scripture how the mystery of God is within each one of us."

Jonathan pointed me to several examples:

- "The kingdom of God is in your midst [or, 'within you']" (Luke 17:21).

- "To [the saints] God willed to make known what is the riches of the glory of this mystery among the Gentiles, which is Christ in you, the hope of glory" (Colossians 1:27).

- "For you have died and your life is hidden with Christ in God" (Colossians 3:3).

- "The Spirit searches all things, even the depths of God. For who among men knows the thoughts of a man except the spirit of the man which is in him? Even so the thoughts of God no one knows except the Spirit of God" (1 Corinthians 2:10–11).

"Orthodox thought supports that the fullness of another person's identity is a secret between them and God. This means that no matter how close I get to someone—I will still only 'see through a glass, darkly' [1 Corinthians 13:12 KJV]. In the book of Revelation we read that Christ will give each person a white stone with a secret name written on it, which only the recipient and God can know. This reveals the intimacy each person possesses with God. It is an intimacy that someone on the outside can only partially know.

"More so, in order for marriage to truly reflect the kingdom of heaven, it must be infused with this mystery. Salvation, in Orthodox theology, is an ongoing participation in the divine nature. We do not arrive—we continue. Even if you don't subscribe to the Orthodox faith, you can see this sense of faith as continuous growth in the concept of sanctification—in the sense that we are continuously invited to grow deeper and deeper with God.

"In the same way, becoming one in marriage is an ongoing journey marked by one of the strongest ingredients of an eternal romance—mystery."

So how does this play out practically in your marriage?

"Mostly, it keeps romance alive and my pride in check. When I begin to think I've got her pegged and I can predict her answers or thought process, I step back and remember the mystery of this woman. Her life is hidden in Christ and even though we are becoming one, there is an inexhaustible mystery to her being.

"Also, people are constantly changing and growing. Rather than fearing this, the Orthodox Church teaches us to embrace growth and transformation. This helps me embrace the mystery of myself as well. Only God fully knows me. Repentance means that I am letting go of my illusions about myself—and embracing the image and likeness of Christ within me. It helps me receive grace for myself, which in turn helps me give grace to my beautiful wife."

READY FOR THE JOURNEY?

I know that for me, this mystery Jonathan speaks of makes the journey of marriage inexhaustibly exciting. Analee and I are in a long and beautiful process of learning each other, becoming one, and cultivating true love. This has a way of invalidating any stagnation or monotony that can creep into a marriage.

So whether we're four years in or twenty, or haven't started yet at all, let's change our minds about love. Love is not something we arrive at and spend our marriages maintaining. As Jonathan alludes, love is a journey marked by mystery and the continual intention to learn one another.

And if you ask me, that's what makes it such an adventure.

COUPLES THAT PLAY TOGETHER STAY TOGETHER

Why Sex Is More Than a Pleasurable Perk of Marriage.

So when the emotions of infatuation fade, are we to simply resolve to a chemical-reaction–free marriage? I certainly hope not. If you do, do so at your own risk because researchers have long understood the secret to keeping a chemical and emotional connection alive and well in a marriage.

But we don't need researchers to tell us, either. What we're talking about, of course, is sex.

Analee's Point of View. *Sex is one of the most beautiful gifts I think God gave us. It makes me sad that so much negativity can* *get tied to the subject. Things like shame and abuse are things that certainly need to be addressed and healing sought out in those areas to experience the redemptive gift of what sex is meant to be with our spouse. There is something so powerful in the vulnerability and beauty we get to share with our spouse. I personally think that it is the best form of stress relief, a way to fight spiritual warfare, and a way to protect your marriage. This most intimate act is designed to knit us evermore into oneness—and it provides many health benefits as well. You can't go wrong. When in doubt, I say, "Have sex."*

During sex—and especially during orgasm—a hormone called oxytocin is released by both parties. As it turns out, this "hormone of love" happens to come with all kinds of side benefits proving that sex is far more than a pleasurable perk of marriage. It's an imperative practice to keeping a long-term connection alive in our marriages.

SEX BONDS.

Prairie voles—small, burrowing mammals that you might see at the zoo—are well-known among the animal kingdom as serially monogamous, making them unique among most other mammals.

I know, this doesn't sound romantic at all—but bear with me a moment.

In a study, these prairie voles were injected with chemicals to neutralize their oxytocin.[32] As a result, these faithful lovers lost all partnership bonding and did not stay together. On the other hand, when oxytocin was injected into prairie voles who were not mating, the same partnership bonding that typically occurs while mating was induced.

Dr. Hans Zingg, a professor at McGill University and a longtime student of the "love hormone," described these results as follows: "There's convincing evidence that oxytocin is involved in mediating stability, pair bonding, and monogamy; the enduring parts of love."[33]

Obviously, we're not prairie voles, and we're not part of a science experiment. So what does this mean for us?

Here's one example. When a test group of people were shown an emotional video documenting a terminally ill cancer victim with his young son, their blood samples showed a 157 percent spike in oxytocin.[34] What's more, their oxytocin levels showed a direct correlation to feelings of empathy.

This experiment and many more all point to the fact that our ability to empathize with others is the basis for all emotional connection. More specifically, oxytocin plays a leading role in our ability to connect to and understand our spouses—and it all starts with sex.[35]

SEX PRODUCES TRUST.

A common practice in the field of psychology is the documenting of the various stages of intimacy in a relationship. Though there's not a universal map to what those stages actually are, all experts seem to agree the most intimate emotional stage requires an excessive amount of trust. This only further proves that years of commitment and supporting experiences are necessary to establish a lasting emotional connection. Yet commitment and years of experience may not be the only thing that can assist in building this kind of trust.

Biologists have observed that humans show abnormal levels of trust after oxytocin is released in our bodies.[36] Interestingly, men and women often try to separate an emotional connection from physical intimacy. Yet science tells another story.

SEX GIVES.

Neuro-economist Paul Zak handed a test group some nasal spray.[37] Half of the bottles were filled with oxytocin, and the other half were filled with salt water. The subjects were then told that they would be given $40 and the chance to give a certain percentage of that money away to another subject, whom they would not meet. Those who snorted oxytocin gave away 80 percent more than those who snorted mere salt water.

Love is not the emotions we feel for our spouse. It's the everyday choices we make to give our lives to them. And it just so happens that sex—by unleashing this incredible force of oxytocin—can make that giving just a bit easier for us.

So the next time your spouse isn't in the mood, feel free to offer them an argument backed by science.

CHAPTER FIVE

YOU, ME, AND EVERYONE WE KNOW

What Happens at Home Doesn't Stay at Home

> *"The happy state of matrimony is, undoubtedly, the surest and most lasting cause of all good order in the world, and what alone preserves it from the utmost confusion."*
> —*Benjamin Franklin*

When I was a kid, I told everybody I wanted to be a "Dowboy." That's cowboy—with a speech impediment.

On most days, you could find me strutting around my house in my fake snakeskin boots (size 4), a brown polyester cowboy hat, and a pair of old jeans with holes in the knees.

I wasn't an outspoken kid. That was mostly because my older sister found it personally gratifying to guess what I was thinking and speak for me. However, when I did talk, I would typically mumble something I picked up from one of *The Young Riders*, my favorite Western show.

The hat and guns were cool to a young wannabe, no doubt. But what really captivated me was that cowboys were always doing something epic. Every episode of an old Western was about a cowboy dueling another cowboy, or protecting his people from danger, or somehow winning his lady's love via an extraordinary act of heroism. I wanted to duel, to protect, to be a hero. I wanted to live that life.

As I grew older, I eventually traded my cowboy boots in for military ones and dreamt of one day serving in the Marine Corps. This eventually faded into hopes of becoming a rock star, then a church pastor, then a social entrepreneur. Yet my reason behind these vocational whims never changed: *I wanted to do something meaningful. I wanted to live an extraordinary life.*

No one dreams about being mediocre as a kid. We want to be firemen or astronauts or wealthy philanthropists. We all dream about doing something important.

Yet when we think about living an extraordinary life, we don't often think of becoming a great husband or wife. As kids, I'm not sure that the idea of faithfully loving a spouse was nearly as captivating as flying jet planes or saving people from raging fires. Even when we're asked to introduce ourselves today, it's far more natural to define our lives in terms of our career. So we talk about our professional title, our work, our projects, and goals. And sure, if we have kids, we'll likely proudly call ourselves parents. But in all this, our role as a husband or wife often takes the backseat.

But I think it's time we reconsider.

Because according to almost every possible measure, being a good spouse is one of the most meaningful and extraordinary and impacting and valuable things we can do in life.[1]

Hard to believe? Let's take a closer look.

YOUR MARRIAGE CHANGES YOUR SPOUSE.

As hard as some of us try, it's challenging to stay the same person after marriage. After all, new responsibilities and radical proximity will always offer more opportunity to grow up. A spouse is like a mirror affording us the chance to frequently see and deal with our stuff. However, in the same way, when the closest person in our lives chooses to love us—despite knowing us—marriage can also show us a powerful image of who we can become.

I like to think of this as a mutual becoming—the phenomenon that happens when committed love removes a spouse's limitations and helps them reach their highest potential.

But the alternate truth to this mutual becoming is that if your spouse is not loved well, he or she may not live out their potential for good in the world. This goes back to the self-developing and empowering realities of true love, as discussed previously, that the apostle Paul alludes to when he tells husbands to love their wives so that her soul might be reformed and so that she might be presented in all her glory.[2]

Psychologist Caryl E. Rusbult echoes a similar pattern in his study of the changing power of love. He says, "Close partners sculpt one another's ideal selves, shaping [each other's] skills and traits and promoting versus inhibiting one another's goal pursuits. As a result of the manner in which partners perceive and behave toward one another, each person enjoys greater or lesser success at attaining his or her ideal self."[3]

In short, as we learn to love and therefore give to our spouse, we not only become the best version of ourselves—we offer our spouse the chance to become the best version of him or herself as well.

Love, then, is giving for the sake of our spouse's becoming.

Yet the impact of marriage doesn't stop there. We're about to see that as we cultivate this kind of love, our kids, our community, and the world enjoy the benefits.

YOUR MARRIAGE CHANGES YOUR KIDS.

John Medina, a molecular biologist and author of *Brain Rules for Babies*, teaches how to raise kids based on the lifetime of research on the development of a child's brain.[4] As you can imagine, he is often approached by adults looking for the silver bullet of parenting. It seems they all want to know one thing: "What's the most important thing I can do as a parent?"

His answer is not what you might expect and it alludes to something I recently stumbled upon.

Remember my home experiment to discover the effect that intentionally loving my wife had on every layer of my life? One particular morning of the experiment, loving my wife had taken a backseat to making sure she got a very real and raw piece of my mind. You know this kind of day. You both wake up seemingly looking for someone to blame.

As we each emphatically "reasoned" with each other as to how the issue was the other's fault, Cruz—our sixteen-month-old son—ran in the room. By all indicators, he looked to be in high spirits on that particular day. Yet by his third step toward us he had picked up on his parents' ensuing chaos. He stopped dead in his tracks. His whole demeanor changed. Then I watched as this seconds-ago happy child proceeded to scream at the top of his lungs and fall to the floor in an all-out meltdown.

Analee's Point of View. *This experience was something that made us reevaluate how we handled conflict in front of our little "sponge" children. Even in my womb, we would tell Cruz,*

"Mommy and Daddy are just disagreeing, but we are okay and we love you." But as tensions increased with career changes, house moves, and having another baby, our intentions lessened. We found ourselves just coping—and forgetting our little human was soaking in everything.

After Cruz's bizarre meltdown, I began wondering about the relationship between our adult tantrums and his own tantrums. So I added an additional observation to my ongoing experiment.

Each day, I rated the health of my marriage on a scale from one to ten. A perfect ten indicated lack of conflict or quick resolution in conflict, several moments of connection throughout the day, and powerful communication.

Then I noted my child's behavior. A ten meant zero tantrums, general pleasantness, and swift obedience. A one, on the other hand, indicated multiple tantrums, mood swings, and strong disobedience.

After thirty-one days, the results confirmed my suspicions. An overwhelming 84 percent of the time, the less connection my wife and I had, the more our child negatively acted out.

As it turns out, my experiment wasn't a fluke. In fact, many have discovered this strong correlation between the parents' marriage and a child's behavior.

But before we take a closer look at this correlation, let me state the obvious and say that single parents or divorced couples are not disqualified from raising great kids. We've all seen parents who don't stay together but continue to raise their kids incredibly well.

On a broad sociological level, however, studies consistently demonstrate that a stable family built on a healthy marriage can make quite an impact on a child's development at every stage of life.

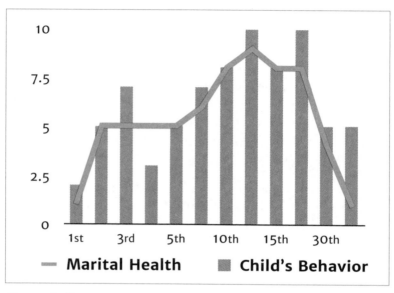

As an infant, stress is far more costly to their tiny bodies than later in life. The constant release of cortisol, adrenaline, and other hormones in response to instability in a home can effectively "wear out" other parts of the brain involved in higher-level thinking. If the stress is prolonged, this can affect the long-term development of a child's attention abilities, impulse control, and fine motor skills.[5]

As a student, kids from a stable home environment are statistically more likely to stay in school, have fewer behavioral and attendance problems, and earn four-year college degrees.[6]

Emotionally, kids with married parents are less vulnerable to emotional illness, depression, and suicide. According to recent research, "In the last half century, the teen and young adult suicide rate has tripled. The single most explanatory variable is the increased number of teens living in a home with divorced parents. The effect is large, explaining as much as two-thirds of the increase in youth suicides over time."[7]

Relationally, kids raised in stable families are more likely to bond more consistently with others, have positive attitudes toward marriage, and have a greater chance of success in forming long-term relationships.[8]

Economically, they are less likely to be poor or to experience persistent financial instability.[9]

All this points to one thing: your marriage has incredible benefits for your children.

But the opposite effect is just as dangerous. According to studies, decreasing marital stability since 1980 is believed to be responsible for:[10]

- An increase of nearly 500,000 children suspended from school
- About 200,000 more children engaging in delinquency or violence
- 250,000 more children receiving therapy
- 80,000 additional children thinking about suicide

To be sure, a single parent can be a successful parent. And I'm well aware that some of the world's best parents have children who face challenges emotionally, relationally, or economically. These statistics aren't to say that every problem a child faces is inherently a parenting issue. They are simply meant to give us pause. When even kids from healthy homes can experience significant challenges, we should be all the more concerned with uprooting our unhealthy patterns in marriage.

Science, on a neurological, behavioral and social level, suggests that every one of us are in some way products of the home environment we grew up in. And the benefits of a healthy marriage to the home environment speak for themselves.

Gary Ezzo and Robert Bucknam, the psychologists behind success-ful child rearing techniques, speak insightfully to this: "A healthy marriage creates an infused stability within the family and a haven of security for a child in their development process."[11] In fact, they even go further by summing up their years of family research as follows: "In the end, great marriages produce great parents."[12]

They're not the only ones to arrive at this conclusion, either.

Reenter John Medina, the molecular biologist, who I had the op-portunity of interviewing.[13] I asked him—joining with thousands of other parents who have posed the same question many times before—"What's the most important thing I can do as a parent for my child?"

His answer, after years of biological research and writing several books on parenting, was instant and simple: "Go home and love your spouse."

And that, as we will soon find, is the most powerful home-brewed recipe for world change.

YOUR MARRIAGE CHANGES THE WORLD.

I used to hate weddings. Though I appreciated the excuse to get down on the dance floor and overload my body with sweets, I gen-erally found them to be a big waste of time and money for the couple. It never made any sense to spend what could be the down payment of your new house just to invite a bunch of friends and acquaintances to witness you say a few vows, exhibit a little PDA, and shove cake in each other's mouths.

My wife said my perspective was unromantic and cave-like. I said it was practical and intelligent. (And, with that, I think I entirely proved her point.)

I found little value in throwing an expensive party to simply show off a highly personal pursuit of two people that really isn't anyone else's business anyway. Yet this idea is a modern and misinformed one.

And as it turns out, I was simply uneducated about this celebration we call a wedding.

John Witte Jr., a renowned legal scholar, blames the era of Enlightenment for this misconception that marriage isn't anyone else's business. Previous to the rise of marriage as a means of personal fulfillment, society largely understood marriage as a means of good for the greater community. As such, it was important to share the wedding ceremony with those it would affect and benefit. Everyone at the time understood what Witte and others continue to argue today: "Marriage is more than a private emotional relationship. It is a social good."[14]

Regardless of our modern overlooking of this social good of marriage, what happens in your home does not stay in your home. What happens in your home has significant implications on your community, your society, and the world.

Your marriage affects society. When the purpose of marriage publicly came under questioning in the early 2000s, Barbara Defoe Whitehead—director of the National Marriage Project at the time—was asked to testify in front of the US Senate. She wrote and then delivered several thousand words explaining the vital importance of marriage to a society. She then called for the public and private sector to explore ways to reduce the barriers to healthy marriage and to make it possible for more parents to form strong and lasting marital unions.

"Being married changes people's lifestyles and habits in ways that are personally and socially beneficial," wrote Whitehead.[15] "Marriage is a 'seedbed' of pro-social behavior."[16]

Whether for better or for worse, your marriage changes the way you behave toward one another, toward your children, and toward your future. And the implications of this changing power ripple far beyond your relationship. "Marriage generates social capital," Whitehead says. "The social bonds created through marriage yield benefits not only for the family but for others as well, including the larger society."[17]

Your marriage affects the economy. Call it unromantic if you must, but the truth is that marriage is a benefit to society in supremely practical ways—including the providing of an economic boost.

"The size of families, and their stability and quality [have] important implications for the health of the global economy," stated the National Marriage Project's director Brad Wilcox in his article for the *New York Times*.[18]

Married couples, for example, build more wealth on average than singles or cohabiting couples. Married men in particular earn more money than do single men with similar education and job histories.[19] In a less tangible way, marriage also changes one's personal goals and behavior in ways that are profoundly and powerfully life-enhancing. As Linda Waite and Maggie Gallagher write in *The Case for Marriage*, "Marriage creates not just a new unit of consumption but a new unit of production: Getting and staying married produces goods for the partners, for their children, and for the rest of society."[20]

Your marriage affects the future of the world. Here is where a marriage's effect on the children comes full circle. Because if the health of your marriage has direct implications for your children's cognitive, emotional, social, and economic health, then you have the incredible ability to shape healthy contributors to a future society.

Modern research demonstrates this, but we can also observe this timeless truth in action at the beginning of history.

The original request God makes of Adam and Eve is to be fruitful and multiply to fill the earth and subdue it.[21] This commission puts marriage right at the center of God's plan not only to influence society, but to create it.

"Marriage is more than your love for each other," says Dietrich Bonhoeffer, the twentieth century German theologian. "It has a higher dignity and power, through which God wills to perpetuate the human race till the end of time. In your love you see only the heaven of your own happiness, but in marriage you are placed at a post of responsibility towards the world and mankind."[22]

So do the world a favor.

Yes, marriage is designed to inspire two people into wholeness.

Yes, marriage can quite possibly become the greatest asset to you and your spouse's life.

And yes, marriage has brilliant intentions in mind—offering you and your spouse all kinds of very real perks in life.

But marriage doesn't stop with just the two of you.

Marriage is an unapologetic and selfless giver. It is innately designed to lead the two of you into an upward, increasing wholeness, and then to offer that dynamic relationship as a gift to the world around it.

Our modern world doesn't need any more Dowboys. It doesn't need more millionaires or leaders or pastors or soldiers or philanthropists—not primarily, anyway.

What the world needs are better lovers—husbands and wives committed to learning the unnatural art of loving another person. What we need are more marriages worth fighting for.

So men, women, the next time you find yourself dreaming about career success, or an epic life adventure, or becoming better parents, or any other way you might dream of living a life of meaning, do the world a favor.

Go home and love your wife. Go home and love your husband.

Because though this art of loving another may be unnatural, it just might change the world.

BONUS CHAPTER

CAVE TALK

Success, Porn, and Other Things Men Must Overcome to Win at Marriage

> *"It was like he was a caveman grunting, 'You woman. Me man. Let's make babies together.'"*
> —Missy Lyons

When we got married, my wife was quick to point out all the ways that modern men are bizarrely similar to ancient cave dwellers. Most of us can't do two things at once. We still hunt and gather—only today we call it acquiring clients or scoring a 401k. When it comes to emotions, many of us still can't seem to navigate without a club. The list goes on.

Men, let's face it. We tend to be the less relationally intelligent party of the marital equation. And as much as I hate to spotlight our gender, several of the modern mentalities that have a way of killing marriages are predominantly subscribed to by men.

Let me also say to the women reading that if I could string together even a sentence of intelligible advice just for a woman, I'd write a chapter for you too. However, the longer I'm married to one of your kind, the less I actually understand your kind.

I do hope, however, that you will find the following thoughts help-ful in understanding your husband and the natural challenges he faces because of his male DNA and society's expectations of him.

However, let's also be mindful that the following couple thousand words can be dangerous in the hands of an irresponsible spouse. We are going to discuss things for men that may make the discrepancy between where your husband currently is in his journey and where you would love him to be quite clear. So before we read on, let's all, husband and wife, agree on a few things.

One. Healthy marriage happens when both parties begin taking 100 percent responsibility for the relationship. I'd suggest applying everything discussed in this chapter to your own life first.

Two. We are all on a journey. Though husbands may tend to be the slower sex when it comes to relational processes, this shouldn't discredit where they are today. Men need a woman's grace for the journey, just as much as you need ours.

Three. Holding this material as a standard over your spouse's head will only make the path to a healthy marriage longer for both of you. I'd recommend against it.

But I digress.

My observations, in my own life and throughout culture, have red-flagged three mentalities that seem to consistently stand in the way of men and a healthy marriage. These three mentalities include misplaced priorities, misinformed definitions of success, and the misadventure of fantasy.

MISPLACED PRIORITIES.

I have a confession to make. I'm a recovering workaholic.

When I say workaholic, I don't necessarily mean the kind who works 100-plus hour weeks. I mean the kind who has made decisions for most of my adult life entirely based on how it affects my work and income—oftentimes to the neglect of far more meaningful areas of life. In other words, my priorities have been dominated by my career—and when it came down to it, if my wife's needs or preferences came in the way of my production at work, work was often the easy choice to make.

Analee's Point of View. *I feel I am very supportive of Ty chasing his dreams and coming alive in his work. Though it was almost as if once he conquered the quest of winning me, he didn't think he'd have to put as much energy into maintaining our relationship. Ty is a very focused individual, and it was and is a challenge for us to find the work/home life balance. We ran into even more challenges becoming parents.*

Unfortunately, we live in a culture that promotes this way of life. If we want to be successful at something, common cultural knowledge suggests, we must make that one thing our deepest passion and top priority—regardless of the cost.

Napoleon Hill, the American writer often attributed as the founder of personal success literature, summarizes our culture's paradigm well: "Because he chose a definite goal, placed all of his energy, all of his will power, all of his effort, everything back of this goal. He stood by it until it became the dominating obsession of his life, burning all bridges behind him."[1]

Napoleon's sentiment here is often applauded as a worthy part of the American Dream. But if you ask me, I think Napoleon missed the point. And I believe we have enough proof to conclude this from the common headlines of so many of our most successful professionals and their deathbed regrets of chasing their career at the cost of relationships.

It's a modern problem, to be sure, but we find the antidote by looking backward into history. As it turns out, these deathbed regrets seem to be legitimized by an ancient king and a modern Jewish rabbi worth listening to.

MARRIAGE > CAREER.

The writer of Proverbs once said, "An excellent wife, who can find? For her worth is far above jewels."[2] This was a shocking statement because jewels in that time were the modern day equivalent of excessive wealth. They were both the means to a life of luxury and the objects worn to prove that life of luxury. The writer, in essence, is claiming that a good spouse—and therefore marriage—is more valuable than money.

Rabbi Shalom Arush tells another story about a young wife he knew who, like Analee, felt like her husband didn't have the time for her and the kids. No matter how many times she would ask, he still never came home from work on time.

The man countered, "Rabbi, believe me that I don't waste time. My schedule is simply jammed from morning until night and urgent situations needing my attention are a commonplace. Is this my fault? And, in the end, my overtime is for the sake of my wife and my kids. I wouldn't come home late unless there was a legitimate reason to."[3]

Rabbi Arush politely let him finish before responding.

"You're dead wrong," the rabbi said. "All of your problems—financial, relational, professional—are because your marriage isn't your highest priority. The gains that a spouse will feel on both a spiritual and material level defy description, once they make their marriage first place."[4]

The rabbi had officially lost me.

I was persuaded that as an entrepreneur, or any professional with career goals, my career must take the throne of my priorities for at least several years. But the rabbi was saying putting my wife first would also bring me professional success. Could it be true?

I assume most of us have our own version of this persuasion. Whether you're a stay-at-home dad simply trying to raise your kids well or a professional focused on putting food on the table, there's always another pursuit—other than our marriage—begging for our primary attention.

I was skeptical of the rabbi's argument. But after observing that putting my work ahead of my marriage had produced little more than paying bills and an unhappy wife, I figured giving Shalom's derailing hypothesis a test drive couldn't hurt.

A CASE STUDY IN PRIORITIES

I made Rabbi Arush's claim my hypothesis for thirty-one days: "If one was to make their spouse feel more important than any other part of their life, they would experience benefits in all other areas of their life."

Then I put the scientific method to good use.

I did the same four things every day to intentionally communicate to my wife that she was more important to me than my career.

One. I would tell her I loved her and one thing I loved about her as the absolute first thing I did each day.

Two. I would reach out to her two to three times during my work-day via call, text, email, Facebook post, or a lunch date.

Three. On the way home from work, I would mentally transition out of work-mode to be able to make her and her day my one fo-cus when home.

Four. I would intentionally emotionally connect with her at least once a day. This often took on the face of a conversation alone, praying together, or sex.

I then measured six different areas of my life on a scale from one to ten every night before I went to bed.

Priority Points. I would earn a perfect ten if I executed all four variables with sincerity (as opposed to obligation). My score would drop from there depending on my lack of execution or intentional-ity. Sadly, you will soon see I have consistency issues.

Quality of Life. A score of ten indicated general happiness and hopefulness about life. A day of stress, pessimism, and short-sightedness was given a one.

Peace in the Home. A score of ten indicated a day of total se-renity in our home, complete with no fights, no meltdowns, and no complaining. A one, on the contrary, alluded to a consistent pres-ence of conflict. You know, "the nights on the couch" kind of days.

Marital Enjoyment. A ten was given when my wife and I wanted to be and enjoyed being around each other. A one was a day spent wanting to stay at work to avoid her and a deep interest in hiding when home.

Career Flow and Productivity. Ten points were awarded for a focused and productive day at work. One point indicated an ADD and unproductive day.

Child's Behavior. I gave the day a ten when my sixteen-month-old son got through the day without exhibiting any unwanted behavior such as meltdowns or tantrums.

If you read chapter 3, you already know how this story ends. After thirty-one days, the evidence spoke for itself: when I make my wife my number one priority, every other area of my life begins to thrive.

See the results for yourself.

The data doesn't lie—and apparently neither does the rabbi. The green line above represents my prioritization of Analee, and you'll notice that every other line seems to follow it. In other words, my entire life experience is influenced by the level of investment I make in my marriage.

Remarkably, prioritizing my wife over my work became the best way to invite her into my work—which then greatly benefited.

Of course, every marriage and every spouse is unique—each with their own variables. Yet this priority phenomenon seems to have some level of truth for every man, regardless of uncontrollable outliers. As the rabbi suggests, "Once a husband invests the time to give a wife the secure feeling of coming first in his life, he's virtually free to do as he pleases. Yet, when the wife lacks that security, the husband will find himself investing hour after hour in trying to placate her."[5]

In the end, we all know work is important. It's not a gender-specific pursuit, either, of course. Both men and women long to do good and meaningful work in a variety of ways. And by no means am I trying to build a case against diligence in our professional pursuits. However, we need to be aware of our propensity to overvalue work at the cost of undervaluing our relationship with our spouse.

So instead of waiting until the end like some of the world's most successful elite, let's get it right now—by putting our marriage first.

MISINFORMED DEFINITIONS OF SUCCESS.

The reality is that my workaholism—our workaholism—doesn't come from nowhere. And to help us put our marriage first over our professional pursuits, we need to better understand why we're motivated to work hard in the first place.

This brings us to the second mentality toxic to husbands today.

Put simply, conventional society often promotes a tragically low, unimaginative mold for success—yet it's a mold many of us are susceptible to.

Suits.

Big houses.

Stage spotlights.

Nice cars.

Picket fences.

Beach homes.

Magazine covers.

Bill Gates.

Brad Pitt.

Mark Zuckerberg.

Unfortunately, this lack of imagination has a trickle-down effect into our personal definitions of success. Whether we recognize it or not, our ideas of success are often simply inherited from others. They may come from our parents, from Hollywood, or from some slightly overweight, middle-aged ad man who drives a red convertible and gets paid far too much to create TV commercials.

Here's the catch. Modern versions of success are overrated and incomplete.

According to the most common dictionaries and—let's be honest—our own opinions, success can be defined as "the attainment of popularity or profit."[6] And though this seems to capture the vision of big homes and Bill Gates, history has already shown us that luxury and fame rarely amount to much of a life.

Don't believe me? Hear it from the rich and famous themselves:

According to Brad Pitt, "Fame makes you feel permanently like a girl walking past construction workers."[7]

"Don't try to be a billionaire," suggests Bill Gates. "It's overrated."[8]

"Fame is overrated," says Keira Knightley, "and it frightens me when kids say 'I want to be famous.' "[9]

Jesus says, "Not even when one has an abundance does his life consist of his possessions."[10]

We all know that money and fame are not inherently bad. We understand the meaningful role finances and influence can play in life. The real issue is that money and fame often make up our entire definition of success—leaving relationships, health, and faith to be slotted in and undervalued.

Once again, we've heard too many deathbed confessions from our brightest, most successful stars about how they wish they would have cared less about their career or money and more about family and friends. We know better than to believe that wealth and fame make a good brand of success.

It's time we intentionally re-architect our definition of success with the health of our marriages in mind.

A DIFFERENT PICTURE OF SUCCESS

As we discussed in chapter 2, the original word describing the relationship between man and woman uses the Hebraic root picture of *esh*, or "fire."

This image evokes a dynamic relationship, and a refining relationship.[11]

Yet there's even more to this image.

The word *Ish*—man in hebrew—is depicted by two pictures, the fire (*Esh*) with the *"yod"* symbol—meaning hand—in the middle of it.

Ishshah—*woman* in Hebrew—is the real hidden gem. It's depicted by a fire—*esh*—with the symbol *"hey"* added on. And in typical Hebrew fashion, when the *hey* comes at the end of the word as it does in *ishshah*, it means to "come out of."[12]

Let's slow down and catch this because the original Hebrew pictorial language has an insightful way of speaking practically to things that are still very relevant today.

A man—within the context of a relationship with a woman—is represented by a hand in the middle of a fire. This seems to suggest that one of his primary roles is to labor in or to tend the fire, or to intentionally foster the relationship.

The word picture for woman within the context of marriage seems to suggest that one of her primary roles is to "come out of" the fire that a man tends.

Two thousand years later, the apostle Paul gives us an even clearer picture (my commentary added): "Husbands, love your wives [tend the fire], just as Jesus also loved the church and gave Himself up for her, so that He might sanctify her . . . that He might present to Himself the church in all her glory [that she may come out of the fire and be presented in all of her glory."[13]

In light of this, we may reconsider our ideas of what it means to be part of this picture. Yes, supporting our wives financially—or in their careers—is important for working men, but it doesn't begin to capture its scope.

Jesus did everything He did, made all the sacrifice He made, so that His bride could experience life "abundantly"[14] and have every opportunity to be a "city on a hill"[15] and be revealed "in all her glory."[16] This was His brand of success. And according to Paul, it's now the brand He passes on to us as husbands.

This definition of success is gauged by how intentionally and intelligently a man invests in his marriage. His success is defined by the fullness of life—the vitality and thriving—of his wife.

If this is true, then our primary question changes. It is no longer, "How can I or my wife get ahead in our careers today to better support our family?" Rather, the question becomes: "What can I do today to make my wife come alive?"

And for all you women still with us, here's a question for you too: "How can I urge my husband on in his own process of development? How can I help him to become the best version of himself?"

THREE QUESTIONS FOR DESIGNING A BETTER LIFE AND MARRIAGE

Once we take a deeper look at our ideas of success, it's easy to see that we may not necessarily want these inherited definitions. I don't know about you, but I don't want to live a carbon copy life of someone else's ideas of success. If that's you too, here are a few questions that may be a helpful starting point in redefining it.

1. *What is success to you?*

Success doesn't have to look the same for everyone. It doesn't have to look like what your family or friends expect. We all function differently, with different gifts and different ideas of what a fulfilling life would look like, so you're free to define success for yourself.

When I discussed these questions recently with some friends, we all approached our answer differently. I redefined success as a simple and local life that is professionally exciting, relationally connected, and spiritually inspired.

Here were some additional pieces of the definitions that came out of our time:

"No matter the income, my work has a sense of purpose and progress."

"My wife has life in her eyes and my kids are emotionally empowered."

"The time and geographic location to foster relationships with people who challenge, encourage, and inspire me, and of whom I can reciprocate the same."

No matter where you are in life, this question can help you evaluate what you want in terms that are more holistic than just the number of digits on your paycheck or the recognition you receive.

Although we also need to be discerning in what is motivating our specific idea of success, which brings us to question two.

2. *Why do you want this brand of success?*

The answer to this question is arguably the most significant layer to redefining success. Being pushed by fear or expectations isn't nearly as powerful as being pulled by purpose and vision.

Again, here are some examples I've come across in recent conversations with friends:

"For the time and energy to invest into my family and friends."

"To offer my wife and children the opportunity to fully experience and enjoy life: education, international exposure, skill training, adventures."

"To take care of friends and family with finances, quality time, a safe place, life wisdom."

"For independence from 'the system' and freedom of choice."

One friend revised a phrase from author Wallace Wattles: "I want to be financially successful to eat, drink, and be merry when it is time to do these things, in order that I may surround myself with beautiful things, see distant lands with my kids, feed my mind, spend time with people I love, and develop my intellect; in order that I may love others and do kind things, and be able to play a good part in helping the world to find truth."[17]

3. What's one thing you're willing to give up for this brand of success?

Any time you set a goal, you can expect resistance in the process of reaching it. Answering this third and final question will help you identify that resistance, hang a target on it, and overcome it before you've even started.

This requires giving something up—any bad habits or attitudes that might be holding you back.

Recent examples I've heard include:

"Obsession with working too much."

"Fear of criticism and preference for hiddenness."

"Need for security and financial control."

"Finding my identity in what I do."

Your idea of success will probably shift many times throughout your life, but thinking through your priorities now will mean the world for your future. Whether you are working your dream job, just trying to get by, or still unsure of exactly what you want to do, take some time to ask yourself these questions to design your brand of success and thus, find a more meaningful expression of life.

THE MISADVENTURE OF FANTASY.

Sadly, most people—both men and women—don't know what sex is today.

Allow me to explain.

It was a fall day in third grade. I jumped off the bus and abided by my normal routine of climbing my next-door neighbor's fence and knocking on the front door to join Jackson, the son of my neighbor's full-time nanny, in whatever nonsense he was getting into that day.

From the moment he opened the door, something about the wild in his eyes and the smirk on his face told me today was different. He anxiously invited me in, quietly shut the door behind me, and ran upstairs. I followed him to the back of the house where a storage closet opened up to a walk-in attic.

Apparently his mom wasn't aware of the dozen boxes of *Playboys* her client was storing when she asked Jackson to organize the attic that day. He wasn't sad about her ignorance, and neither were my preteen hormones. We spent the next sixty minutes skimming the magazines, saying goodbye to innocence, and creating misconceptions about sex that would take me years to understand.

My earliest sexual awakening was built on fantasizing about women who weren't actually real. These bad ideas about sex continued to be facilitated by the occasional exposure to pornography throughout my teenage years. And even though I never developed an addiction, my exposure was enough to keep me thoroughly misinformed about sex.

Most men have their own version of this story. According to the most recent statistics in 2013, 85 percent of men look at pornography at least once a month.[18] But whether you're currently part of the 85 percent or not, you've most likely been misinformed about sex by marketers and the media machine all throughout your life.

1. Fantasy vs Sex

Pornography has lied to us about sex. It elicits and perpetuates ideas about intimacy that are actually more about fantasy than they are about real sex. Porn has taken a gift given to us to cultivate a lasting relationship and turned it into an act of self-fulfillment.

In fact, there are many ways porn has—both subtly and significantly—stolen from the meaning, beauty, and long-term benefits of sex for most men today.

2. Conquest vs Connection

The woman on that computer screen requires nothing more than that you look at her. And though conquering her in your mind may somehow make you feel validated, there's nothing truly validating about it.

Sex is so much more than some physical conquest or achievement. It's designed to facilitate real, holistic connection—mind, body, and spirit. And though this artificial validation porn offers can be addictive, the holistic connection of real sex offers so much more than a momentary high.

"The complete physical and emotional proximity of sexual inter-course," says Mary Anne McPherson Oliver, "is the single most im-portant factor in the creation of the couple's unity and deeply, ir-revocably, and continually alters the people involved."[19]

It's no secret that if a man has any bit of explorer in him, it doesn't take long to experience every part of his wife's body. And sure, she may not always be as open and inviting as digital companions por-tray themselves—but she's far more excitingly dynamic, far more human, than pixelated beauty can ever be. What your wife offers you are the true benefits of sex. These benefits aren't limited to the ecstasy of an orgasm—but include the physical, emotional, and spiritual connection that is cultivated with the person we get to wake up next to tomorrow morning.

3. Escaping vs Engaging

"Porn is not about sex," Paula Hall, a sexual psychotherapist, says. "A man doesn't need to look at pornography for six or seven hours if he just wants sexual gratification. It's about escapism. It's a se-cret world they can disappear into, as many addictions are."[20]

On the contrary, sex in marriage requires that we actually show up. And not just with our bodies, but with our whole selves—physi-cally, emotionally, spiritually, and psychologically. Sadly, these ar-tificial sexual experiences that seem to effortlessly remove us from our world of stress and uncertainty have been said to make real sex not feel worth the effort and vulnerability.

The truth is that artificial sex offers little more than a brief escape followed by a harsh return to the same stressful and uncertain reality.

In contrast, the effort and vulnerability involved in sex with your spouse is an investment with an incredible return. It offers holistic intimacy, rather than the emotional emptiness of porn. And while it is an effective stress-reliever, it also creates a long-term reality in your marriage and family that you likely won't want to escape any time soon.

4. Pleasure vs Love

You offer nothing to that woman on the screen. She, on the other hand, offers you the chance to feel validated, to escape, and to indulge yourself with a few moments of pleasure. Therefore, your alleged experiences with her make the intentions of sex entirely about you and what you can get from her.

But real sex is designed with a different intention in mind.

Sex is scientifically proven to be one of the more effective cultivators of intimacy in marriage. As one expert puts it, "There's convincing evidence that oxytocin [the hormone released during sex] is involved in mediating stability, pair bonding, and monogamy; all the enduring parts of love."[21]

It's this enduring kind of love—real love, with a real woman—that's worth abandoning fantasy for. And let's make no mistake about it, you can't have both.

NINE REASONS TO STAY AWAY FROM PORN

If not confronted, this addiction to fantasy can become a consuming fire threatening all quality of life. So before you go looking again for that woman on the screen, here are nine reasons to consider against it.

1. Porn makes you unhappy and bored

Research says that those who regularly indulge themselves in pornography are more likely to have higher levels of anxiety and depression and lower levels of self-esteem than those who don't. The brain is to blame for this.[22]

Apparently, as one artificially stimulates the pleasure center of their brain with porn, it perpetually weakens in its ability to respond to natural kinds of pleasure. Before we know it, real life has to compete with the unnatural and artificial levels of chemical excitement that porn offers. Real life—and our marriage—often lose this competition.

Pamela Paul, the author of *Pornified*, puts it this way: "Pornography leaves men desensitized to both outrage and to excitement, leading to an overall diminishment of feeling and eventually to dissatisfaction with the emotional tugs of everyday life . . . Eventually they are left with a confusing mix of supersized expectations and numbed emotions . . . and become imbued with indifference. The real world often gets really boring."[23]

Sex with our wives proves to be quite a different story. The natural chemicals and pleasure real sex creates doesn't inflate our expectations or numb our emotions. According to studies performed by the Institute for the Study of Labor, real sex actually makes us happier.[24] The same studies also show that married people have more sex than those who are not married, and even experience far higher levels of satisfaction in life.[25]

2. Porn neuters you

Some people believe that pornography can add excitement to their sex life. However, studies prove just the opposite. Porn actually produces less intimacy between partners, less romantic excitement, and less satisfaction in real sexual experiences.[26]

Dr. Mary Anne Layden writes in *The Social Cost of Pornography*, "I have also seen in my clinical experience that pornography damages the sexual performance of the viewers. Pornography viewers tend to have problems with premature ejaculation and erectile dysfunction. Having spent so much time in unnatural sexual experiences with paper, celluloid and cyberspace, they seem to find it difficult to have sex with a real human being."[27]

Because of pornography, men have trouble getting turned on by their wives who happen to not be cybersex slaves. As a result, they don't enjoy real sex nearly as much as they used to. This is because porn makes us less satisfied with our partner's affection, physical appearance, and sexual performance.[28]

On the contrary, when porn isn't a part of marriage, real sex proves to only get better with time. Sociologist Mandi Norwood discovered this socially unenforced reality after interviewing several hundred women. She found that married women are satisfied in the bedroom because of years of practice, less inhibitions, and the time to learn their partner.[29]

3. Porn is not manly

Though conquering that woman on the screen in your mind may make you feel like a man, there's nothing manly about it.

Real sex involves you. All of your fears. All of your insecurities. All of your capacity to give. It also involves another very real person. All her needs. All of her baggage. All of her propensity to judge you and hurt your dignity.

Porn requires no work, no sacrifice, and no maturity. Real sex in marriage requires you to risk, to be vulnerable, to give yourself fully to another person. This kind of intimacy is not for boys. It's for men only.

4. Porn doesn't make friends

Studies show that men who use porn commonly become isolated from others, highly introverted, narcissistic, dissociative, and distractible.[30] In other words, it doesn't exactly make you a likeable person.

Neurochemistry teaches that the more that you bond with fantasies on your computer screen, the harder it is to actually bond with real people. This is because the strongest bonding substance in our lives is oxytocin—the hormone released during orgasm. As this powerful bonding substance becomes consistently associated with porn, it becomes easier for us to feel connected in fantasy than it is in reality.

Porn kills human connection. And human connection is what relationship lives and dies by.

5. Porn is a professional liability

Pornography is the master of preoccupation. According to recent polls, 18 percent of men who view porn regularly admit to be distracted by it even when not online, and 30 percent acknowledge that their work performance suffers because of this distraction.[31]

In striking contrast, research also proves that across the board, men who have a healthy sex life make more money than those who don't.[32]

You decide what's better.

6. Porn hurts your wife

It's easy to think that your porn habit is private, and doesn't affect anyone but you. Yet as we've already seen, porn inevitably kills a man's ability to emotionally connect and consistently monopolizes his desires.

Whether your wife knows you are using pornography or not, your actions have already hurt her.

Rabbi Arush puts it this way: "A woman is not just a body, but a vibrant soul that thrives on intimacy, attention, communication, consideration, respect, and the love of two souls binding together. A husband that focuses on his own physical gratification doesn't provide his wife with any of the emotional and spiritual gratification that is the basis of her vitality."[33]

7. Porn will turn you into "that guy"

You know "that guy." Most crowds have at least one. He's the one who cares about no one but himself. He sees you and all others as commodities to be used, not people to be cared for. No matter how much you can't stand "that guy," as long as you continue to dabble in porn, you run the risk of becoming him.

Gail Dines puts it bluntly in her book *Pornland*. "In the story of porn, men are soulless, unfeeling, amoral life-support systems... who are entitled to use women in any way they want. These men demonstrate zero empathy, respect, or love for the women they have sex with."[34]

No one wants to be "that guy." What's more, no one wants to be with "that guy" who only sees women as consumable objects and cares for no one but himself.

8. Porn will never actually do it for you

"Just as Twinkies are artificially enhanced," says the nonprofit team Fight the New Drug, "and modified food that really aren't good for you, pornography is an artificially enhanced and modified sexual experience that isn't good for you either, and your body knows it."[35]

Lust, in its nature, is never satisfied. It only wants more.

9. Porn will kill your marriage

In the eight reasons above, we've looked to science, social studies, and history to witness the effects that pornography has on those who entertain it. We've seen that it kills everything long-term love is built on: human connection, trust, and self-sacrifice. It's no wonder, then, that at least 56 percent of divorce cases today involve one party who compulsively visits pornographic websites.[36]

Your marriage may survive your habit for a period of time. However, if you continue to choose fantasy over reality, it will inevitably destroy your ability to love your wife.

As modern men, we certainly have plenty of unnatural things to navigate to keep our marriages healthy and alive. However, my hope is that—with a vision of a marriage that is worth fighting for—we're more determined than ever to do just that.

NOTES

CHAPTER ONE: A PICTURE WORTH FIGHTING FOR

1. "Marriage and Divorce Statistics," Avvo, 2009, http://www.avvo.com/legal-guides/ugc/marriage-divorce-statistics.

2. Slater & Gordon, "Marriage Meltdown," July 10, 2013, http://www.slatergordon.co.uk/media-centre/press-releases/2013/07/marriage-meltdown-slater-and-gordon-commission-report-on-the-modern-marriage/.

3. Jessica Bennett, "The Case Against Marriage," *Newsweek*, June 11, 2010, http://www.newsweek.com/case-against-marriage-73045.

4. Andrew Cherlin, The Marriage-Go-Round: The State of Marriage and the Family in America Today, *Vintage*, April 6, 2010, as quoted in: Jessica Bennett, "The Case Against Marriage."

5. "Marriage and Divorce Statistics," Avvo, 2009, http://www.avvo.com/legalguides/ugc/marriage-divorce-statistics.

6. Bennett, "The Case Against Marriage."

7. This section is simply stating facts derived from research on the topic of marriage and divorce. These topics, however, are clearly much more complicated than just data and statistics.

8. The information cited here is derived from polling those who have never married, as well as those who are divorced. The purpose of these statistics is to show the benefits of marriage by itself—not to compare it with the benefits of singleness.

9. Linda J. Waite and Maggie Gallagher, *The Case for Marriage: Why Married People Are Happier, Healthier, and Better Off Financially* (New York: Broadway Books, 2001), 133, 135, 173, 197, 280.

10. Ibid., 171–73.

11. Phillip Moeller, "Why Marriage Makes People Happy," *U.S. News and World Report*, March 22, 2012, http://money.usnews.com/money/personal-finance/articles/2012/03/22/why-marriage-makes-people-happy, excerpted from *How to Live to 100: Be Happy, Be Healthy, and Afford It* (*U.S. News & World Report* ebook, 2012).

12. Waite and Gallagher, *The Case for Marriage*, 200.

13. Tyler Ward, "3 Things I Wish I knew Before We Got Married," *RELEVANT*, January 23, 2013, http://www.relevantmagazine.com/life/relationships/3-things-i-wish-i-knew-got-married.

14. Niels Bohr, as quoted by Edward Teller, "Dr. Edward Teller's Magnificent Obsession" by Robert Coughlan, *LIFE* magazine, 6 September 1954, 62.

CHAPTER TWO: CARVING TO THE SKIN

1. Stanley Hauerwas, "Sex and Politics: Bertrand Russell and 'Human Sexuality'," *Christian Century*, April 19, 1978, 417–22, http://www.religion-online.org/showarticle.asp?title=1797.

2. Genesis 3:16.

3. Hara Estroff Marano, "The Expectations Trap," *Psychology Today*, March 1, 2010, http://www.psychologytoday.com/articles/201003/the-expectations-trap.

4. Brad Wilcox, "Is Love a Flimsy Foundation? Soul-mate versus Institutional Models of Marriage," *Social Science Research* 39, Issue 5 (2010): 687–99.

5. John Leggett and Suzanne Malm, *The Eighteen Stages of Love: Its Natural History, Fragrance, Celebration and Chase* (Lanham, MD: Rowman & Littlefield Publishers, 1995), 139, accessed in http://www.cbc.ca/news2/background/science/chemistry-of-love.html.

6. It's only a legend, though many accounts claim that the stone did, in fact, sit in the marketplace for over fifteen years before Michelangelo took it home. Read more at http://www.italian-renaissance-art.com/Michelangelo-David.html.

7. Inspired by "The Michelangelo Phenomenon" by Caryl E. Rusbult, Eli J. Finkel, and Madoka Kumashiro: http://faculty.wcas.northwestern.edu/eli-finkel/documents/47_RusbultFinkelKumashiro2009_CDir.pdf.

8. Genesis 2:23.

9. You can view the symbol here: http://www.biblestudytools.com/lexicons/hebrew/nas/esh.html.

10. Mark 9:49.

11. Zech. 13:9 ESV.

12. Psalm 66:12.

13. Ephesians 5: 25–27.

14. From the Greek word for salvation," *sótéria*, http://www.biblestudytools.com/lexicons/greek/nas/soteria.html.

15. Linda J. Waite and Maggie Gallagher, *The Case for Marriage: Why Married People Are Happier, Healthier, and Better Off Financially* (New York: Broadway Books, 2001), 171.

16. Dan Allender and Tremper Longman, *Intimate Allies: Rediscovering God's Design for Marriage and Becoming Soul Mates for Life* (Carol Stream, IL: Tyndale House Publishers, 1999), 288.

17. Philippians 2:12.

18. Proverbs 27:19.

19. Shalom Arush, *The Garden of Peace: A Marital Guide for Men* (Austin, TX: Diamond Press, 2008), 45.

20. Kathleen and Thomas Hart, *The First Two Years of Marriage: Foundations for a Life Together* (Mahwah, NJ: Paulist Press, 1983), 50.

21. Arush, *The Garden of Peace*, 60.

22. Ibid., 17.

23. Marina Benjamen, "Marriage Myth: Spouses Can't Change," accessed on February 1, 2014, http://psychcentral.com/lib/marriage-myth-spouses-cant-change/00021.

24. Jared Black writes at JaredEthanBlack.com.

CHAPTER THREE: REAL ROMANCE

1. Tara Blanv, "The Myth of the Perfect Marriage," accessed February 1, 2014, http://psychcentral.com/lib/the-myth-of-the-perfect-marriage/00010528.

2. Inspired by John Witte Jr., *From Sacrament to Contract: Marriage, Religion, and Law in the Western Tradition* (Louisville, KY: Westminster John Knox Press, 1997), 209, as quoted in Tim Keller, *The Meaning of Marriage* (New York: Dutton, 2011), 50.

3. Ibid.

4. The Declaration of Independence: http://www.archives.gov/exhibits/charters/declaration_transcript.html.

5. Daniel Lapin, *Thou Shall Prosper: Ten Commandments for Making Money* (Hoboken: Wiley, 2009), 246.

6. Ephesians 5:25 MSG.

7. Ann Voskamp, "The Real Truth about 'Boring' Men—and the Women who Live with Them: Redefining Boring," *A Holy Experience*, November 15, 2013, http://www.aholyexperience.com/2013/11/the-real-truth-about-boring-men-and-the-women-who-live-with-them-redefining-boring/.

8. Otto Piper, *The Biblical View of Sex and Marriage* (New York: Scribner, 1960), 134.

9. Acts 20:35.

10. See Galatians 6:7–8; Luke 6:38; Job 4:8; Hosea 10:12–13.

11. Shalom Arush, *The Garden of Peace: A Marital Guide for Men* (Austin, TX: Diamond Press, 2008), 45.

12. Vilfredo Pareto, *Cours d'Économie Politique Professé a l'Université de Lausanne*, vol. I, 1896; vol. II, 1897, as referenced in Tim Ferris, *The 4 Hour Work Week* (New York: Harmony, 2009), 244.

13. Read the full interview at tylerwardis.com/Gary-Chapman-Interview

14. Read the full interview at tylerwardis.com/Gary-Thomas-Interview

CHAPTER FOUR: ONE + ONE = ONE

1. Nicole Tomlinson, "The Chemistry of Love and Attraction," CBC News, February 14, 2008, http://www.cbc.ca/news2/background/science/chemistry-of-love.html.

2. Helen Fisher, *Why We Love: The Nature and Chemistry of Romantic Love* (New York: Holt Paperbacks, 2004), as referenced in http://www.cnn.com/2007/LIVING/personal/10/09/end.relationship/

3. Song of Solomon 1:2–4 MSG.

4. John Leggett and Suzanne Malm, *The Eighteen Stages of Love: Its Natural History, Fragrance, Celebration and Chase*, 139, as accessed at http://www.cbc.ca/news2/background/science/chemistry-of-love.html.

5. "Marriage and Divorce Statistics," Avvo, 2009, http://www.avvo.com/legal-guides/ugc/marriage-divorce-statistics.

6. Linda J. Waite and Maggie Gallagher, *The Case for Marriage: Why Married People Are Happier, Healthier, and Better Off Financially* (New York: Broadway Books, 2001).

7. Full Interview with Gary Thomas can be read here: tylerwardis.com/gary-thomas-interview.

8. Genesis 2:24 KJV.

9. Here is just a small sample of other material available on this topic: *The Seven Levels of Intimacy* by Matthew Kelley; *The Couple's Journey* by Susan Campbell; *Love after Marriage* by Barry and Lori Byrne; *The 7 Stages of Marriage* by Rita M. DeMaria and Sari Harrar; *Building a Reality-Based Relationship* by Liberty Kovacs. Neither the author nor the publisher is endorsing everything in all of these resources. The discerning reader should proceed accordingly. Mary Anne McPherson Oliver, *Conjugal Spirituality* (Franklin, WI: Sheed & Ward, 1994), 56.

10. Charles Williams, *Descent into Hell* (Grand Rapids, MI: Eerdmans, 1949), 130, as quoted in Mary Anne McPherson Oliver, *Conjugal Spirituality* (Franklin, WI: Sheed & Ward, 1994).

11. Quoted in Oliver, *Conjugal Spirituality*, 35. As referenced in: Gary Thomas, *Sacred Marriage* (Grand Rapids, Michigan: Zondervan, 2008).

12. Ibid., 38.

13. A. Pascual-Leone, A. Amedi, F. Fregni, and L.B. Merabet, "The Plastic Human Brain Cortex," *Annual Review of Neuroscience*, (2005): 28, 377–401.

14. Ibid., 35.

15. Ibid., 39.

16. Oliver, *Congugal Spirituality*.

17. Entire interview with Ray Ortlund can be read here: tylerwardis.com/ray-ortlund-interview.

18. Oliver, *Conjugal Spirituality*, 41.

19. Ibid.

20. Read the full interview with Jared Black here: tylerwardis.com/jared-black-interview.

21. Oliver, *Conjugal Spirituality*, 35.

22. Ibid.

23. http://www.amazon.com/s?ie=UTF8&field-author=David%20Augsburger&page=1&rh=n%3A283155%2Cp_27%3ADavid%20Augsburger.

24. Gary Smalley, *Making Love Last Forever* (Nashville: Thomas Nelson, 1997), 144.

25. As referenced in Gary Thomas, *Sacred Marriage* (Grand Rapids, MI: Zondervan, 2008), 376.

26. Read all of the interview here: tylerwardis.com/byrnes-interview and learn more about *Love After Marriage* at http://www.loveaftermarriage.org/cms/.

27. See Lori and Barry Byrne, *Love After Marriage* (Ventura, CA: Regal, 2012), 98–100.

28. Read all of the interview with Paul here: tylerwardis.com/paul-young-interview.

29. Lori and Barry Byrne, *Love After Marriage*, 101.

30. Ibid., 106.

31. Read the full interview with Jonathan Jackson at tylerwardis.com/jonathan-jackson-interview.

32. Nicole Tomlinson, "The Chemistry of Love and Attraction," *CBC News*, http://www.cbc.ca/news2/background/science/chemistry-of-love.html.

33. Ibid.

34. Paul J. Zak, "The Moral Molecule," *Psychology Today*, November 22, 2009, http://www.psychologytoday.com/blog/the-moral-molecule/200911/the-science-generosity.

35. Tomlinson, "The Chemistry of Love and Attraction."

36. Ibid.

37. Zak, "The Moral Molecule."

CHAPTER FIVE: YOU, ME, AND EVERYONE WE KNOW

1. Linda J. Waite and Maggie Gallagher, *The Case for Marriage: Why Married People Are Happier, Healthier, and Better Off Financially* (New York: Broadway Books, 2001).

2. Ephesians 5:25–27.

3. Caryl E. Rusbult, Eli J. Finkel, and Madoka Kumashiro, "The Michelangelo Phenomenon," *Current Directions in Psychological Science 18* (2009): 305.

4. More about John Medina: http://www.johnmedina.com/.

5. Petersen Wittmer, "The Effects of Stress and Violence on Brain Development," Education.com, July 20, 2010, http://www.education.com/reference/article/effects-stress-violence-brain-development/.

6. Barbara DaFoe Whitehead, "Healthy Marriage: What It Is and Why Should We Promote It?" presented at the Senate Hearing, April 28, 2004, http://www.gpo.gov/fdsys/pkg/CHRG-108shrg93523/html/CHRG-108shrg93523.htm.

7. David M. Cutler, et al, "Explaining the Rise in Youth Suicide," Working Paper 7713 (Cambridge, MA: National Bureau of Economic Research, May, 2000).

8. DaFoe Whitehead, "Healthy Marriage: What It Is and Why Should We Promote It?"

9. Robert Lerman, "The Impact of the Changing U.S. Family Structure on Poverty and Income Inequality," *Economica 63* (1996): S119–S139.

10. Paul R. Amato, "The Impact of Family Formation Change on the Cognitive, Social, and Emotional Well-Being of the Next Generation," *The Future of Children* 15 No. 2 (2005), 89. Also referenced here: http://futureofchildren.org/futureofchildren/publications/docs/15_02_05.pdf.

11. Robert Bucknam and Gary Ezzo, *On Becoming Baby Wise* (Sisters, OR: Parent-Wise Solutions, 2001), 21.

12. Ibid., 21.

13. Read full interview here: tylerwardis.com/john-medina-interview.

14. Linda J. Waite, "Does Marriage Matter?" *Demography 32* No. 4, (1995): 28.

15. DaFoe Whitehead, "Healthy Marriage: What It Is and Why Should We Promote It?"

16. Ibid.

17. Ibid.

18. Bradford Wilcox, "Strong Marriages and Economies," *New York Times*, January 19, 2012, http://www.nytimes.com/roomfordebate/2011/10/16/fewer-babies-for-better-or-worse/strong-marriages-strong-economies.

19. Waite and Gallagher, *The Case for Marriage*, 29.

20. Ibid.

21. Genesis 1:28.

22. Dietrich Bonhoeffer, *Letters and Papers from Prison* (New York: Touchstone, 1997).

BONUS CHAPTER: CAVE TALK

1. Napolean Hill, *Think & Grow Rich* (Winston-Salem: Fortune Publishing Group, 2013), 20–21.

2. Proverbs 31:10.

3. Shalom Arush, *The Garden of Peace: A Marital Guide for Men* (Austin, TX: Diamond Press, 2008), 64.

4. Ibid.

5. Ibid., 70.

6. Oxford Dictionary, http://www.oxforddictionaries.com/us/definition/american_english/success.

7. Brad Pitt Quotes, http://voices.yahoo.com/18-greatest-quotes-brad-pitt-273327.html.

8. Todd Bishop, "Gates to Students: Don't Try to Be a Billionaire, It's Overrated," *Geekwire*, October 27, 2011, http://www.geekwire.com/2011/gates-tells-uw-students-billionaire-overrated/.

9. "Knightley Criticises Fame-Seekers," *BBC NEWS*, August 21, 2007, http://news.bbc.co.uk/2/hi/entertainment/6956348.stm.

10. Luke 12:15.

11. Special thanks to Jared Black for his insight on this.

12. Genesis 2:23.

13. Ephesians 5:25–27, paraphrased.

14. John 10:10.

15. Matthew 5:14.

16. Ephesians 5:25–27.

17. Wallace D. Wattles, *The Science of Getting Rich* (Pendell, PA: Quincentenntial Publishing Company, 2012).

18. "Pornography Statistics: Annual Report 2013," http://www.covenanteyes.com/pornstats/.

19. Mary Anne McPherson Oliver, *Conjugal Spirituality* (Franklin, WI: Sheed & Ward, 1994), 64.

20. Barbara Davies, "A Few Clicks of the Mouse, and Internet Porn Destroys Yet Another Middle-Class Marriage," *Daily Mail*, February 11, 2009, http://www.dailymail.co.uk/femail/article-1141485/A-clicks-mouse-internet-porn-destroys-middle-class-marriage-.html.

21. Nicole Tomlinson, "The Chemistry of Love and Attraction," *CBC News*, http://www.cbc.ca/news2/background/science/chemistry-of-love.html.

22. William M. Struthers, *Wired for Intimacy: How Pornography Hijacks the Male Brain* (Downers Grove, IL: InterVarsity Books, 2009), 64–65.

23. Pamela Paul, *Pornified: How Pornography Is Damaging Our Lives, Our Relationships, and Our Families* (New York: Times Books, 2010), 90–91.

24. "Having More Sex Than Their Peers Makes People Happy: Study," *New York Daily News*, April 17, 2013, http://www.nydailynews.com/life-style/health/sex-peers-happy-article-1.1319041.

25. Ibid.

26. Jennings Bryant and Dolf Zillmann, eds., *Pornography: Research Advances and Policy Considerations* (New York: Routledge, 1988).

27. Mary Eberstadt and Mary Anne Layden, *The Social Costs of Pornography: A Statement of Findings and Recommendations* (Princeton: The Witherspoon Institute, 2010).

28. Bryant and Zillmann, *Pornography: Research Advances and Policy Considerations.*

29. http://www.dailymail.co.uk/femail/article-180374/Does-marriage--better-sex.html.

30. Struthers, *Wired for Intimacy*, 64–65.

31. "Can Porn Use Affect Memory and Concentration?" http://yourbrainonporn.com/can-porn-use-affect-memory-and-concentration.

32. "People Who Have Sex at Least Four Times a Week Make More Money," *Huffington Post*, http://www.huffingtonpost.com/2013/08/14/more-sex-higher-wages_n_3755271.html.

33. Arush, *The Garden of Peace*, 43.

34. Gail Dines, *Pornland: How Porn Has Hijacked Our Sexuality* (Boston: Beacon Press, 2010), xxiv.

35. "What Porn Really Is," http://www.fightthenewdrug.org/Science/Articles/Synthetic-Sexuality-What-Porn-Really-Is/.

36. "Pornography Statistics: Annual Report 2013," http://www.covenanteyes.com/pornstats/.

Other Moody Collective Books

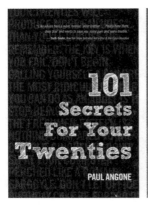

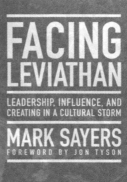

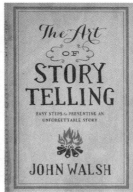

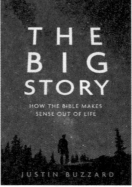

moody
collective

Join our email newsletter list to get resources and
encouragement as you build a deeper faith.

Moody Collective brings words of life to a generation seeking deeper faith. We are a part of Moody Publishers, representing this next generation of followers of Christ through books on creativity, travel, the gospel, storytelling, decision making, leadership, and more.

We seek to know, love, and serve the millennial generation with grace and humility. Each of our books is intended to challenge and encourage our readers as they pursue God.

When you sign up for our newsletter, you'll get our emails twice a month. These will include the best of the resources we've seen online, book deals and giveaways, plus behind-the-scenes and extra content from our books and authors. Sign up at *www.moodycollective.com.*

a part of Moody Publishers